James McDougall

Geography of Palestine

James McDougall

Geography of Palestine

ISBN/EAN: 9783337293840

Printed in Europe, USA, Canada, Australia, Japan

Cover: Foto ©Andreas Hilbeck / pixelio.de

More available books at **www.hansebooks.com**

GEOGRAPHY OF PALESTINE:

HISTORICAL AND DESCRIPTIVE.

ON A NEW AND COMPETITIVE SYSTEM,

FOR YOUNG PEOPLE IN SCHOOLS AND FAMILIES.

BY

JAMES McDOUGALL,

PASTOR OF THE BROUGHTON CONGREGATIONAL CHURCH,
MANCHESTER.

WITH MAP.

LONDON:
SIMPKIN, MARSHALL, AND CO. LIMITED, STATIONERS'
HALL COURT;
SUNDAY SCHOOL UNION, 56, OLD BAILEY.
MANCHESTER: J. BROOK AND CO., 33, HOPWOOD AVENUE;
MANCHESTER AND SALFORD SUNDAY SCHOOL UNIONS.

[*All Rights Reserved.*]

1895.

INSCRIBED,

WITH KINDEST REGARDS,

TO

MY OLD AND FAITHFUL FRIEND,

MR. JOHN MATHER, F.C.A.,

BEECH HOUSE, HIGHER BROUGHTON,

MANCHESTER.

PREFACE.

THE purpose of this Manual is (1) to give children and young people, whether at school or at home, some reliable knowledge of Palestine as the theatre of the history of the Hebrew nation, and of the earthly Life and Ministry of the Lord Jesus Christ; (2) to fix this knowledge permanently in their minds by means of a pleasant and stimulating system of imparting it; and (3) to create an appetite for the continued study of the historical and descriptive geography of the Holy Land.

The following is the system : Using the latest and best authorities, "Statements" have been prepared, varying from three to fifteen lines in length, each statement containing one or more facts or items of information respecting a province, district, locality, site, scene, city, village, or natural feature of the Holy Land, expressed in clear, concise, and simple words.

The Text is divided into Sections, the statements being numbered consecutively.

The scholars forming a class learn the statements by heart and recite them to the teacher. When, say, a hundred statements have been thus learned and recited, what is called

A STRIVE

may take place.

A STRIVE consists of the free, unprompted recital of statements by the scholars, in rotation, as they stand or sit round a map of Palestine. The first scholars are required to recite the five statements in the first Section.

In reciting a statement a scholar, pointer in hand, advances to the map, names the province, district, site, city, village, or natural feature to which the statement he is about to repeat refers, points it out, and then returns to his place.

After the first five statements have been recited, the scholar next in order may recite any statement he pleases. Scholar by scholar, and statement by statement, the "Strive" proceeds until someone repeats a statement already used, or assigns a statement erroneously to the place he or she has mentioned, or fails to repeat correctly the statement selected. In any of these cases the competitor falls out of the class, and takes no further part in the "Strive." As the "Strive" advances, one after another falls out until there remains only one competitor, who is required to say one more unrecited statement, and this done he or she is declared the winner.

For the orderly conduct of the "Strive," a secretary (or secretaries) is appointed, who sits at a table near the map and records the number of each statement recited. Any challenge as to a statement being correctly repeated, or as to its having been used before, is at once settled by referring to the secretary.

Many teachers in Sunday and Day-schools, who have been present at meetings convened for the illustration of this system, are prepared to bear witness to its value and success. It has been explained, and practically exemplified in public, by request of the Committees of the Manchester and Salford Sunday School Unions, who furnish adequate evidence of their approval of it by authorizing the publication of this Manual under their auspices.

The map which accompanies the Manual is the largest of the maps in Major Conder's volume on Palestine, in Messrs. George Philip and Son's series of "The World's Great Explorers and Explorations," and is used by arrangement with that firm.

GENERAL INDEX OF SECTIONS.

	PAGE
PALESTINE—Physical Features	1
,, Name, Settlement, and Divisions	2
,, Coast	2
PLAIN OF ESDRAELON	3
MARITIME PLAIN	4
SHEPHELAH	5
NEGEB OR SOUTH COUNTRY	5
VALLEY OF THE JORDAN	5
RIVER JORDAN	6
GALILEE	9
TOWNS AND SITES ON SHORES OF THE SEA OF GALILEE ...	12
INLAND TOWNS AND SITES OF GALILEE	19
SAMARIA	28
PLAIN OF SHARON	39
JUDÆA	40
JOPPA OR JAFFA	42
TOWNS AND SITES ON THE SHEPHELAH ...	43
PHILISTINE AND SAMSON COUNTRY	45
DAVID COUNTRY	49

GENERAL INDEX OF SECTIONS.

	PAGE
COUNTRY OF THE PATRIARCHS	51
HEBRON AND ITS SURROUNDINGS	53
NORTHWARD FROM HEBRON THROUGH THE WILDERNESS OF JUDÆA	56
MAR SABA AND SOLOMON'S POOLS	58
BETHLEHEM	59
JERUSALEM	65
JERUSALEM AS IT IS	75
MOUNT OF OLIVES AND BETHANY	82
JERUSALEM TO JERICHO	86
JERICHO AND DISTRICT	88
DEAD SEA	93
RIVERS FLOWING FROM THE EAST INTO THE JORDAN	95
PERÆA	96
DECAPOLIS	97
PHŒNICIAN SITES AND CITIES	98

INDEX OF STATEMENTS.

Abarah (Beth-abarah) ... 45	Beirout 11, 124, 189-191, 644
Abraham, 206, 207, 226, 236, 301, 382, 388, 398, 470	Beisan 174
	Beit-lahm 457
Abel-Meholah 596	Belus, River... 679
Absalom 397, 555	Berachah, Valley of ... 418
Aceldama 554	Beth-abarah ... 45, 177
Acre 672-676	Bethania 177
Adam, near the Jordan ... 616	Bethany 570-583
Adullam, Cave of .. 360-361	Bethaven 240
Ænon 46	Bethel 235-240
Ahab ... 194, 195, 199	Bethesda, Pool of ... 541-542
Ai (el Tel) 241	Beth-Hogla 613
Ain-el-Haniyeh 339	Bethlehem 249, 434-468
Ain-Harod 178	Road from, to Jerusalen 469
Ain-Jenin 680	Valley of 471
Akka (Acre) 673	Bethoron 502
Amos 416	Beth-phage 576
Andrew ... 102, 109, 524	Bethsaida 109-112
Annunciation, Place of the 150	Bethshan 174-177
Antonia, Fortress of 510-512	Bethshemesh 351-352
Aphek 122	Bezetha 507
Apostles' Well 585	Bent-Sheikh Lot 627
Araunah, Threshing Floor of 369	Bir-el-Khat 585
Arimathæa 561	
Ark, The Hebrew 332-335, 351-352	Cæsarea 11, 273-286
Arnon, River ... 630-631	Cæsarea Philippi .. 191, 669-671
Ascalon 336	Callirhoë 629
Ascension of Christ, Place of 583	Calvary 556-558
Ashdod 334	Cana 138-139
	Capernaum 77-92
Babylon, Jews' Captivity in 496-497	Lake of... 78
	Fountain of 107
Balata 207	Carmel, Mount ... 259-272, 682
Banias 37	Chedorlaomer 668
Baptism of Jesus 48	Cherith, Brook 591
Bar-Cochba 527	Chorazin 108
Bartimæus 602	Cities of the Plain ... 624-625
Beatitudes, Mountain of the 133	Cornelius 276
Beeroth 244-247	Crocodile River 286
Beersheba 380-389	
Wells of ... 384-387	Dalmanutha... 94-95

INDEX OF STATEMENTS.

Damascus ... 124, 338, 640
Damascus Gate, Solomon's
   Quarries near 540
David 358, 360, 396, 402, 486
David Country,
   Method of Ploughing in 357-371
David's Well 442
Dead Sea 619-628
Decapolis, Region of 640-643
Disciples of Jesus 64
Dorcas 311
Druses, The... 665

Ebal, Mount 216, 220-222, 228
Ebenezer 352
Ekron 331-332, 335
Elah, Valley of 358
El-Bireh (Beeroth) 244
El-Harathiyeh 188
Eli, the High-priest ... 233
Elijah, 42, 170, 171, 266-270, 301,
   389, 596, 664, 682
Elisha, 42, 43, 239, 271, 596, 362,
   612
   Spring of 597
El-Jish 181
El-Kalil 398
El-Lisan 623
El-Mouhrattah 268
El-Ram 248
El-Tel (Ai) 241
Emmaus 559-560
Endor 166-167
En-Gannin 680
Engedi 422-424
Ephraim 601, 602, 639
Ephrath 437
Er-Riha 594
Eschol, Valley of 398
Esdraelon, Plain of... 10, 12-20
Etham 429-430
Et Tabigah, Bay of... 105-107
Evil Counsel, Hill of 474, 564

Fik, Gorge of 122

Gadara 120, 121
Galilee 54-67
   Upper 67-70
   Lower 71
Galilee, Sea of 72-76

Galilee, Sea of—
   Industries of people
   living around the 113-114, 117
   Water of 100
   Pickled Fish of ... 117
   Width of 118
Gath 333-335
Gaza 337-338, 340 345
Gehenna 553
Gennesaret, Land of 123-124
Gerar 373-379
Gergesa 118-119, 642
Gerizim, Mount ...220-226, 228
Gethsemane, Garden of 568-569
Ghor, The ... 33-35, 40, 624
Gibeah 242-243
Gibeon 484-485
Gihon, Valley of ... 475-476
   Pools of 477
Gilboa Hills ... 18, 19
Gilead, Mount 17
Gilgal 224, 610, 613
Giscala 182
Goad, The 291
Goats 377-378
Golgotha 556-558
Gomorrah 624
"Gordon" Site of the Cruci-
   fixion 557-558

Harosheth of the Gentiles... 188
Hasbany, River ... 37, 677
Hazazon-Tamar 424
Hebron 390-413
   Road from, to Jerusalem 412-
   413
Hebron Valley 390
Herod Agrippa 190
Herod Antipas ... 97-98
Herod, the Great 185, 284, 454.
   506-510, 513
Hermon, Mount ... 666-667
Hinnom, Valley of 471, 475, 553
Hippicus, Tower of ... 509
Houses, Flat-roofed 460-462-463
   With Stairs 461
Huleh, Lake, or "Waters
   of Merom" ... 183-186

Isaac... ... ... 373, 382

INDEX OF STATEMENTS.

Jabbok, River ...630, 632, 633
Jabesh, Men of ... 176
Jabneh ... 66
Jacob 208, 226, 237, 238, 633
Jacob's Well 210, 216
Jalud, Mount ... 17
James ... 92, 250
Jebel-es-Sheikh ... 666
Jebus ... 479
Jebusites ...479, 480-483
Jehoshaphat, Valley of ... 475
Jericho ... 594-618
    Road from Bethany to 584-585
    Plain of ... 593
    Fall of ... 618
Jeruel, Wilderness of ... 418
Jerusalem ... 469-559
    Seven Hills of ... 478
    David's Work in ... 486
    Solomon's Work in ... 487
    Solomon's Temple 489-492
    Water Supply of ... 492
    Revolt of Ten Tribes 493-494
    Siege of, by Nebuchadnezzar 496
    Return of Jews to ... 497
    Rebuilding of 498
    Internal Quarrels ... 499
    Herod's Work in 506-515
    Walls and Towers of 507-512
    Herod's Temple at 513-523
    Siege of, by Titus 524-526
    Under Constantine ... 528
    Modern City ... 532-524
    Christ's Triumphal Entry into ... 577
    Christ Weeping over ... 581
Jeshimon ... 417
Jesus Christ, 47, 48, 61, 77, 83, 84, 89, 90, 91, 92, 94, 99, 111, 112, 119, 135, 136, 142, 145, 152, 154, 155, 158, 160, 211, 212, 228, 247, 250, 251, 252, 257, 303, 310, 343, 415, 444, 445, 448, 450, 472, 511, 516-523, 542, 546, 548, 559, 568, 572-574, 577-583, 586, 601-603, 628, 638, 639, 641, 642, 651, 652, 667, 671
Jews' Captivity in Babylon 496-497
  ,, Cemetery ... 555

Jezreel, Plain of ... 12
John the Baptist 45-49, 111-597, 609, 628
John the Evangelist 92, 250, 256
Jonah ... 310
Joppa or Jaffa ... 304-318
Jordan, Valley of 29-34
    Called the Ghor ..33-35
Jordan, River 35-53
    The Name ... 36
    Pride or Swelling of ... 40-53
    Three Dividings of ... 42
    Fords of ... 44
    Place of Baptism of Jesus 47
    Water used for baptisms 50
    Crossed by the Israelites 615-616
Jordan, Plain of ... 51
Joseph ... 394
Joseph's Tomb ... 229-231
Joshua 209, 221, 232, 326, 395
Judas Maccabæus ... 502
Judas, Tree of ... 564
Judæa, Physical Features of 294-303
    Harvest Operations in 368
    Modes of Travelling in 414-415
    Shepherd's Life in ... 420
    Wild Animals in ... 421
    Historical Associations 303

Kadesh ... 187
Kedron, Valley of ... 475
    Stone Bridge over the... 567
Kefr Birim ... 131
Kefr Kenna ... 138-140
Keraseh ... 108
Khan Hathrur ... 586
Khan Minyeh ... 79, 81
Khersa 108, 118-119
Kirjath-arba ... 392
Kishon, River or Brook 677, 680-682
Kurn Hattin 132-137

Lebanon Range 141, 142, 665, 668
Leontes, River ... 662, 677
Lot's Wife... ... 625-627
Luz 235-237
Lydda ... 312, 318, 320-328

INDEX OF STATEMENTS.

Maccabees, The	...329, 501-505
Machærus, Castle of	628-629
Machpelah, Cave of	403-407
Magdala	93-95
Mamre	... 392
Oak of	407-409
Mar Elyas	259, 468
Maritime Plain	21-23
Mariamne, Tower of	... 509
Mar Saba	426-428
Mary	145, 150, 151, 156, 158, 247, 343, 415, 443, 444, 445, 450
Mary Magdalene	... 93
Mattathias	... 501
Matthew, the Evangelist	85, 86
Megiddo, Plain of	... 12
Meiron	129-131
Mejdel	... 93
Merom, Lake	183-187
Milk Grotto, The	450-451
Moabite Stone, The	... 634
Modin	329, 501
Moreh, Hill of	... 172
Moriah, Mount	489, 538
Naaman	... 43
Nachal, The	... 475
Nablus	219, 220, 227
Nain	159-160
N'aman, River	677-679
Nathaniel	... 138
Nativity, Church of the	446-447
Grotto of the	446-449
Nazarene, the title	... 153
Nazareth	141-158
Negeb, The	... 26-28
Oak of Abraham, or Mamre	208, 407-409
Œlia Capitolina	... 527
Offence, Mount of	... 474
Olive, The	363-367
Olives, Mount of	.. 474, 562-583
Omar, Mosque of	... 538
Palestine, Physical Features of	1-5
Its Name, Settlement, and Divisions	.. 6-11
Tribal Divisions of	8
Provinces of	9
Coast of	11

Palestine—	
Flowers of	... 14
Palm, The	425, 593, 594, 598, 599, 600
Patriarchs, Country of	... 372-411
Paul, the Apostle	181, 253, 279-283, 512, 653
Peni-el	... 633
Peræa	636-639
Peter	102, 109, 112, 256, 276, 277, 312, 322
Phasaëlus, Tower of	... 509
Philip	109, 254-256, 338
Philistine and Samson Country	330-356
Phœnicia	644-681
Plague, The	... 23
Precipitation, Mount of	... 157
Ptolemais	... 674
Quarantania, Mount	590-591, 608-609
Rachel, Tomb of	249, 469
Ramah	248-249
Ramleh	323-325
Rantieh	... 325
Rehoboam	... 496
Rephaim, Valley of	.. 471
Ruth	... 439
Safed	125-129
Salt, Pillars of	626-627
Samaria, Province of	201-204, 258, 259
City of	192-200, 254-256
Samaritan, Parable of the Good	257, 586
Samaritans, The	223-228, 230, 250-253
Samson	344-349
Sanhedrin, The	66, 180
Sarepta	...659, 662-664
Saul, King	...167, 176, 242
Scopus, Mount	... 475
Scythopolis	... 175
Sepphoris	... 66, 179-180
Sepulchre, Church of the Holy	537
Sharon, Plain of	287-293
Rose of	... 290
Shechem	...205-210, 258

INDEX OF STATEMENTS.

Shechem—
    Valley of .. 217-218
Shefa 'Omr 678
Shephelah, The 10, 24-25, 319
Shepherd's Sling 359
Shepherds' Field 452
Shepherds keeping watch
    over their flocks ... 372
    Putting forth the Sheep 374
    Leading the Flocks ... 375
    Their Care for the Lambs 376
Shepherds of Bethlehem ... 464
Shiloh 232-234
Shittim, Plain of ... 51, 614-615
Shunem 168-173
Sidon 645-659
Siloam, Pool of ... 543-548
    Village of 549
    Royal Gardens near ... 550
Simon the Tanner's House 313
Sisera 161
Sodom 624
Solomon 476, 485, 487, 489-493
Solomon's Pools ... 431-433
    Quarries 540
Sorek, Valley of ... 351, 357
South Country, The ... 371
Surah 346
Sycamore Fig-tree 355, 356, 603
Sychar 212

Tabernacle, The ... 232-233
Tabor, Mount ... 161-165
Tarichæa 115-116
Teben 354

Tekoa 416-417, 419
Tel Hûm 79-80
Temple of Herod ... 513-524
    Jesus in the ... 516-523
Temple of Solomon.. 489-492
Ten Tribes, Revolt of 493-494
Threshing Floors 369
Tiberias 96-104
Tibneh 326, 328, 329
Timnath-serah 326
Torah 346-348
Transfiguration of our Lord 667
Tyre 648, 650-651, 655-662
Tyropœon Valley 488

Urtas 429-430
Umm-el-Jerrar 373

Virgin, Fountain of the 551-552

Way of the Sea, The ... 82
Wady-es-Sunt 358
Wady-Kelt 587-593
Wady-Semak 643
Wailing Place, Jews' ... 539

Yahmur, The 265
Yarmuk, River ... 630-635

Zacchæus 603-607
Zaherany, River 659
Zaretan 615-617
Zarpath (Sarepta) 663
Zerka, River 286
Zion, Mount 483

GEOGRAPHY OF PALESTINE.

PALESTINE.

PHYSICAL FEATURES.

1. **Palestine** is beyond all other countries the most memorable in the history of the human race; it is also the most important because of its sacred sites, scenes, and associations.

2. Palestine has no great cities; no great rivers flow through its valleys; it has no commercial renown; it never had a standing army or navy; compared with other countries it has been one of the humblest and the poorest; but because it was the home of God's chosen people—Israel, and the birth-land of JESUS CHRIST, it is more renowned and revered than any of the great empires of the world.

3. Palestine is the southernmost part of Syria, extending from the mountains of Lebanon on the north to Idumæa on the south, and from the Mediterranean Sea on the west to the Syrian desert on the east.

4. Palestine consists of four physical portions, or strips, running north and south between the sea and the desert. These are the Maritime Plain, the Central Range of hills, the Valley of the Jordan, and the Highlands forming its eastern border.

5. The peculiar formation of Palestine constituted a strong natural defence against every enemy, and well-fitted it to be the home of a people destined to receive and preserve a Divinely-revealed religion.

NAME, SETTLEMENT, AND DIVISIONS.

6. PALESTINE has been so called from the Philistines who took it from the ancient Canaanites. Thus PHILISTIA became the Gentile name of the land in the form of PALESTINE.

7. About the year B.C. 1920 the descendants of Abraham, consisting of the sons of Jacob, or Israel, their families and dependants, went down into Egypt, where they dwelt for about 400 years. Then, by command of Jehovah, Moses brought them out by the way of the Red Sea, through the south country and the land of Moab, northward, to a spot on the other side Jordan, south-east of Jericho.

8. When the Israelites entered Palestine, it was apportioned to them in parts corresponding with their tribes. One part was given to each of the following tribes: SIMEON, REUBEN, GAD, JUDAH, BENJAMIN, DAN, EPHRAIM, ISSACHAR, ZEBULUN, NAPTHALI, ASHER; MANASSEH was divided, and separate portions were given to the half-tribes bearing that name.

9. Anciently divided between the sons of Jacob, Palestine was in our Lord's day divided into three Provinces, viz.: GALILEE in the north, SAMARIA in the middle, and JUDÆA in the south.

10. Besides its principal Divisions, Palestine has several natural features of importance, the chief of which are the PLAIN OF ESDRAELON, which breaks in two the central range of hills and forms the south-western portion of Galilee; the MARITIME PLAIN; the SHEPHELAH, or low hills lying between the Maritime Plain and Judæa; and the Negeb, which lies south-west of Judæa, and is in Scripture called the south country or the south.

11. With the exception of Beirout, which is beyond Sidon in the extreme north, and Cæsarea and Joppa, which are between the Bay of Acre and its southernmost point, the whole coast of Palestine is singularly devoid of harbours. Dr. George Adam Smith describes it as "merely a shelf for the casting of wreckage and the roosting of sea-birds."

THE PLAIN OF ESDRAELON.

12. The **Plain of Esdraelon** begins at the sea-coast under the northern slope of Mount Carmel, and after following the course of the range southward and eastward sweeps on to the Valley of the Jordan, which it unites with the Maritime Plain. According to Major Conder, the north-western portion of this great plain bears the name of Jezreel and the south-eastern portion the name of Megiddo.

13. The PLAIN OF ESDRAELON presents an unbroken surface of fertile soil,—soil so good that when the land was originally divided amongst the sons of Jacob, the tribe of Issachar consented to pay tribute for it. The blessings promised to Jacob and Moses seem to be inscribed on the face of this wonderful plain.

14. It is from such fertile plains as that of Esdraelon, from such fair fields as those of Nazareth, Nablus, and Bethlehem; and from some of the rich pasture-lands of Judæa that Palestine obtains its fame as a land of flowers. They grow wild, too, on seemingly bare mountain sides and in rocky crevices; they "stand in regiments" in the depths of great gullies after the winter rains, and "now and then a spare acre of soil is all ablaze with scarlet poppies."

15. The remarkable fertility of Esdraelon is largely due to a constant supply of water. In winter springs burst from the ground and send forth copious streams; and even in summer Esdraelon has its fountains, round which the thickets keep fresh and green.

16. When the Midianites invaded Palestine 3,000 years ago, they had their head-quarters in the eastern portion of the Plain of Esdraelon, because there they commanded ample supplies for their horses, camels, and herds of cattle. There they "lay along in the valley," as the story of Gideon tells, "like grasshoppers for multitude, and their camels without number." (Judges vii. 12.)

17. The spot whence Gideon and his three hundred men started on their divinely-ordered expedition against the Midianites was Mount Gilead, now called Mount Jalud, a part of the mass of the Gilboa Hills. The scene of his

victory must have been near the descent of the Plain towards Bethshan.

18. At the eastern end of the Plain of Esdraelon rises the Gilboa range—not one simple mass, but "a network of hills," the highest peak being 1,693 feet above the sea-level. By no means devoid of beauty, the whole range is bare, its once numerous trees having been gradually destroyed partly by herds of goats and partly by charcoal-burners.

19. It was in his lamentation for the death of Saul and Jonathan in the disastrous battle of Gilboa, David uttered the terrible imprecation : "Ye mountains of Gilboa, let there be no dew nor rain upon you, neither fields of offerings ; for there the shield of the mighty was vilely cast away, the shield of Saul not anointed with oil." (2 Samuel i. 21.)

20. Like the Maritime Plain the PLAIN OF ESDRAELON was frequently the "cock-pit" of armies, and for similar reasons, namely, its comparatively level surface and the great highways leading to and through it. Of these roads the two most important were those which traversed Jezreel in the west and Megiddo in the east.

THE MARITIME PLAIN.

21. **The Maritime Plain** was, and indeed still is, intersected by the main roads that traverse Palestine to and from Egypt and the south ; Cæsarea, Esdraelon and the north ; Samaria, the Sea of Galilee and the north-east ; Jerusalem, Jericho and the east.

22. From its situation, its comparatively level surface and its open coast, the Maritime Plain became the regular route of embassies and armies. It was the battle-field, too, of Egyptian, Persian, Assyrian, Grecian, and Roman rivals and invaders; after them, of the Crusaders and Saracens. Later still, only a century ago, indeed, Napoleon the Great led an army into Palestine by its great south road, only to retreat as others before him had done ; like them, too, after failure, the burning of towns and granaries and the massacre of prisoners.

23. Besides being the historical highway of merchants and invaders, the Maritime Plain was also the road by which the PLAGUE entered Palestine from its native place— the Delta of Egypt.

THE SHEPHELAH.

24. **The Shephelah** lies between the Maritime Plain and the hill-country of Judæa. As you approach it from the coast "you see a sloping moorland break into scalps, and ridges of rock, and over these a loose gathering of chalk and limestone-hills, round, bare and featureless, but with an occasional bastion flung well out in front of them."

25. The Shephelah was the scene of conflicts between Israel and the Philistines; later, between the Maccabees and the Syrians; and, later still, between the Saracens and the Crusaders.

THE NEGEB OR SOUTH COUNTRY.

26. **The Negeb** is an uudulating region comprising the Wilderness of Beersheba, and some other contiguous districts mentioned in the Old Testament. From its highest point it sinks eastward towards the Desert of Judæa, and southward by bold steps towards the Desert of Sinai.

27. The soil of the Negeb is red in colour and very rich, producing excellent crops of corn and pasturage. It rests upon a formation of soft white marl.

28. The word NEGEB really means the dry or parched land, for there are in it few visible sources of water, and in the hot season everything comes to look as if it were burnt. But it has many artificial wells, the most interesting of which are those of BEERSHEBA.

THE VALLEY OF THE JORDAN.

29. The most remarkable feature of Palestine is the **Valley of the Jordan,** which intersects the country from north to south, in a line nearly parallel with the sea-coast, at a distance from it in the north of barely 35, and in the south of not more than 50 miles.

30. The length of the Jordan Valley from the Waters of Merom (Lake Huleh) in the north to the Dead Sea is 100 miles; from the Sea of Galilee to the Dead Sea it is 65 miles.

31. At LAKE HULEH the Jordan Valley is seven feet above the level of the Mediterranean; but from that place it rapidly sinks, so that soon after it starts again from the southern point of the Sea of Galilee it is 682 feet, and when it reaches the Dead Sea it is actually 1,292 feet below the Mediterranean level.

32. The width of the Jordan Valley varies from three to fourteen miles. For thirteen miles after leaving the Sea of Galilee its breadth is about four miles; at Bethshan it is between six and seven miles; from Bethshan, being pressed in by the Samarian hills, it narrows to three miles; then the hills gradually recede and it widens to eight miles; further south it expands to fourteen miles, which is its width at Jericho.

33. The portion of the Valley of the Jordan between the Sea of Galilee and the Dead Sea is usually called the GHOR, an Arab name. It is filled with brushwood of Tamarisk, a plant called Vitex Agnus Castus, and other flowering shrubs.

34. Owing to the almost torrid heat of the Ghor and the ample supply of water provided by many little mountain streams, its vegetation is of tropical richness and beauty.

THE RIVER JORDAN.

35. Down the GHOR, at a depth of 150 feet, between banks and cliffs of white marl, there courses and twists the most celebrated river in the world—**the River Jordan;** sometimes a sparkling torrent, sometimes hidden beneath bushes and cane-beds.

36. Immediately below the Sea of Galilee the descent of the Jordan is over 40 feet a mile, and the impetus thus given to a large volume of water, in a very narrow bed, causes a great rapidity of current. Hence the name of the river, YAR'DEN—JORDAN—literally "the down comer."

37. The Jordan has its source near BANIAS, a little place on the slopes of Mount Hermon. It immediately joins the little river Hasbany, and, united, they flow onward in one stream.

38. The width of the Jordan varies with the season; sometimes it is not many yards, but in high flood, the whole Ghor is under water.

39. The volume of water in the Jordan is greatest when the snows on Hermon begin to melt, about the time of Passover, when "Jordan overfloweth its banks all the time of harvest," for harvest in this deep valley is much earlier than even in the plain of Sharon (Josh. iii. 15).

40. To any one who surveys from the hills any great stretch of the GHOR or Jordan bed, the river seems to trail and wind about like an enormous serpent, the rank jungle-growth giving it a deep green colour. In the Old Testament this was spoken of by Jeremiah as the "Pride of Jordan," but it was generally used as a symbol of danger and trouble.

41. Although the Jordan could never be considered a serious defence against invaders, it was to the Hebrews a sacred and even a mysterious river. The crossing of its narrow stream by Joshua and the tribes, on entering Canaan, was as great an event in their history as the crossing of the Red Sea.

42. The Old Testament records three "dividings" of the waters of the Jordan; the first when the tribes passed over to enter the Promised Land (Joshua iii.); the second when Elijah smote the stream with his mantle (2 Kings ii. 8); the third when Elisha smote it with the same mantle on his return to his prophetic work (2 Kings ii. 14).

43. Only once in Scripture do we read of the waters of the Jordan being used for a miraculous and healing purpose, namely, when, at the command of Elisha, Naaman, the Syrian general, who was a leper, washed seven times in them and was healed of his disease (2 Kings v. 10).

44. THE FORDS OR CROSSING-PLACES OF THE JORDAN are many; some of them of great historical interest, especially those mentioned in the Bible. No fewer than 40 crossing-places have been found by the surveyors of the

Palestine Exploration Fund, only a small number of which were previously known.

45. The most interesting of the Jordan fords is at a spot a little north of Bethshan, and called by the natives ABARAH, place of crossing. This is probably that BETH-ABARAH where John baptized (John i. 28).

46. Besides Beth-abarah, ÆNON is mentioned as a place where John the Baptist preached and baptized. Ænon is said to have been "near to Salim" (John iii. 23), the site of which has not yet been ascertained.

47. At one of the crossing-places of the Jordan, Jesus was baptized of John; "And straightway coming up out of the water, he saw the heavens opened, and the Spirit like a dove descending upon him: And there came a voice from heaven, saying, Thou art my beloved Son, in whom I am well pleased" (Mark i. 10-11).

48. At or near the place where he had baptized Jesus, the next day John saw Jesus coming to him again, and pointing Him out to the multitude said, "Behold the Lamb of God, Who taketh away the sin of the world" (John i. 29). After bearing further testimony to the Mightier One, "the latchet of whose shoe he was not worthy to unloose," John added the solemn declaration, "And I have seen, and have borne witness that this is the Son of God" (John i. 34).

49. Beginning his ministry in the wilderness of Judæa, John the Baptist called the people to repent. He presented himself in the garb of the ancient prophets (Matt. iii. 4; Mark i. 6) and employed similar language to theirs. Having attracted many by his preaching he led them to the Jordan, where he baptized them, and never afterwards left its banks until arrested and put in prison.

50. Often since the baptism of Jesus in the Jordan, royal and less exalted families have obtained water from that famous river for baptismal purposes. Our own Queen has provided Jordan water for the baptism of every one of her children, grand-children, and great grand-children.

51. The plain on the eastern side of the Jordan, opposite the Plain of Jericho is called the Plain of Shittim, and sometimes the Plain of Jordan. Between the two plains the

Jordan runs swiftly on its way to the Dead Sea, which is only a few miles distant. On both sides is a fringe of rich vegetation, consisting of stretches of reeds "shaken in the wind," little woods of acacias, oleanders, and tamarisks in which nightingales, bulbuls, and countless turtle-doves find delightful homes and abundant food.

52. The sides of the channel, through which the Jordan flows to the Dead Sea, show that it has had several banks rising one above another in terraces. The highest of these terraces allowed a stream of water sixteen miles wide, so that once the river, at high flood, swept behind Jericho. A second terrace reached to the Spring of Elisha; and a third to about a mile from the present banks.

53. "Descending the steep face of the present banks of the Jordan," writes Dr. Geikie, "to a depth of over 50 feet, we are in the midst of a bird-paradise of acacias, willows, silver-poplars, and other trees. Here, too, is a dense undergrowth of reeds and plants. This part of the channel is the 'swelling' (Jeremiah xii. 5) or 'pride of Jordan,' once the haunt of the lion, and still of the leopard and wild swine. When a flood takes place the waters sweep up to the terrace above, driving out the wild beasts in terror of their lives."

GALILEE.

54. The name, **Galilee,** which recalls so many of the most sacred memories of our race, means nothing more than "the ring." Galil is anything that rolls, or is round.

55. The name Galilee was first given to the northern border-land of Palestine. In Isaiah's time it included the region of Gennesaret. In the time of the Maccabees it extended to the Plain of Esdraelon, and so covered the whole of the northern province of Palestine, which has ever since been called Galilee.

56. The population of NORTHERN GALILEE, always largely Gentile, was in our Lord's time more Gentile than before. Hence the appropriateness of the title given to it, "Galilee of the Gentiles" (Matt. iv. 15).

57. Galilee is bounded by Phœnicia on the north-west; by Lebanon on the north; by Lake Merom, the Jordan and

the Sea of Galilee on the east; and on the west by the Mediterranean Sea.

58. Galilee is the best-watered province of Palestine, a fact due to the mountains of Lebanon on its northern border which, besides feeding the Jordan, send forth smaller streams which irrigate the land.

59. In our Lord's time Galilee was a very different province from that which it is to-day. Josephus describes it as having a rich and well-cultivated soil, with fruit and forest trees of all kinds in plenty; numerous large cities and villages, amounting in all to no less than 240, while the number of inhabitants was nearly three millions.

60. Remains of splendid synagogues still exist in many of the old towns and villages of Galilee, showing that from the second to the seventh century of our era the Jews were numerous and prosperous.

61. Galilee was the scene of the greater part of our Lord's private life and public acts. His infancy, boyhood, and early manhood were spent in Nazareth; and when He entered on His great work He made Capernaum His home.

62. It is a remarkable fact that the first three Gospels are chiefly taken up with our Lord's ministry in Galilee, while the Gospel of John deals more especially with His ministry in Judæa.

63. The nature and character of our Lord's parables were greatly influenced by the features, occupations, and productions of the country; the corn-fields, the fishing trade, the merchants, and the flowers, were appropriate to Galilee; while the vineyard, the fig-tree, the shepherd, and the desert-pathway in the parable of the Good Samaritan were equally appropriate to Judæa.

64. Eleven of the first twelve disciples of Jesus Christ were Galileans by birth; only one of them—Judas Iscariot, the betrayer, having been a native of Judæa. Hence the reason of the contempt manifested for them, as well as for their Lord and Master, by the proud and insolent Judæans.

65. On the destruction of Jerusalem by the Romans, Galilee became the chief place of residence of the Elders and Rulers of the Jews, and of their most celebrated Rabbis.

66. The Sanhedrin, or National Council, assembled for a time at Jabneh, or Jamnia, in the Philistine country, for safety, but soon removed to Sepphoris, and afterwards to Tiberias, where the Mishna was compiled by Rabbi Judah Hakkodesh about the year A.D. 109; and a few years afterwards the Gemmorah was added.

67. Galilee was usually divided into two regions—UPPER and LOWER GALILEE.

68. UPPER GALILEE embraced the whole mountain-range between the upper Jordan and Phœnicia; its southern border ran along the foot of the Safed range from the northwest point of the Sea of Galilee to the Plain of Akka, now called Acre.

69. Upper Galilee, according to Josephus, extended from Bersabe, on the south, to the village of Baca, on the borders of the land of Tyre, on the north; and from Meloth, on the west, to Thella, a city near the Jordan, on the east. None of these places are now known, but the natural boundaries of the Province are easily recognised.

70. The mountain-range of Upper Galilee is an extension of the Lebanon, from which the deep ravine of the river Leontes separates it. The summit of the range is tableland, beautifully wooded with oak trees and tangled shrubbery of hawthorn and arbutus. The district is varied by fertile glens, green forest glades, and picturesque valleys running from east to west.

71. LOWER GALILEE included the great Plain of Esdrselon and its offshoots. These ran down to the Jordan, several miles south of the Sea of Galilee. It also included the hill-country, which extended from the northern shore of the sea to the Lebanon range. It was thus one of the most beautiful sections of Palestine.

72. THE SEA OF GALILEE is one of the most interesting features of Palestine. Sweet water full of fish, a surface of sparkling blue which seems to tempt down breezes from above, this wonderful lake is at once food, drink, and air, a rest to the eye, coolness in the heat, an escape from the crowd, and a welcome means of travel in so exhausting a climate.

73. The Sea of Galilee lies in a torrid basin, where the atmosphere is generally hot and heavy. When cold currents of air passing from the west are sucked down in gusts through the narrow gorges that open upon the sea, they create the sudden storms for which the region is notorious.

74. The inhabitants of Galilee were very proud of their splendid lake. The Rabbis used to say, "Jehovah hath created seven seas, but the Sea of Gennesaret is His delight."

75. To-day the Sea of Galilee is a quiet and even melancholy lake. Its one town, Tiberias, is a poor place of 6,000 inhabitants. Round all the coast there are only three or four villages. Strange to say there are no native farmsteads, and only one or two German farms and crofts. The lights that come out at night on shore and hill are the camp-fires of wandering Arabs. A boat with a sail is seldom seen on its waters.

76. The shores of the Sea of Galilee were very different when Christ came down from Nazareth to find His home and His disciples there. There are no trees where once great woods grew; marshes fill the places of noble gardens; and but a boat or two where once were fleets of sails.

TOWNS AND SITES ON THE SHORES OF THE SEA OF GALILEE.

77. **Capernaum**—KEPHAR NAHUM—THE VILLAGE OF NAHUM—is the name of a city with which all are familiar as the scene of many incidents and mighty works in the life of our Lord and Saviour Jesus Christ. Capernaum is not mentioned in the Old Testament.

78. Little is certainly known of the exact site of Capernaum. It was on the northern shore of the Sea of Galilee, not far from the spot where the Jordan flows into the sea; and, if recent discoveries may be trusted, it was in our Lord's time of sufficient importance to give to that sea, in whole or in part, the name of the "Lake of Capernaum."

79. Two spots are in dispute as the probable site of Capernaum, namely, (1) KHAN MINYEH—a mound of ruins, evidently an old Khan near the sea-shore, at the north-west

extremity of the Plain of Gennesaret; and (2) TEL HÛM, a spot where ruins of walls and foundations cover half-a-mile of the surface, about three miles from the point where the Jordan enters the sea.

80. The principal ruins at Tel Hûm are those of the "White Synagogue," so called because it was built of white lime-stone. Colonel Sir Charles W. Wilson says of this building, "If Tel Hûm be Capernaum, this is without doubt the Synagogue built by the Roman Centurion, and one of the most sacred places on earth."

81. Dr. George Adam Smith says the evidence is greatly in favour of Khan Minyeh as the true site of Capernaum, and adds, "One may fix the house of Jesus, as Mark calls it, the birth-place of the Gospel, at that north-east corner of fair Gennesaret, where the waves beat now on an abandoned shore, but once there was a quay and a busy town, and the great road from east to west poured its daily stream of life."

82. The "WAY OF THE SEA"—a title used in Scripture —was the great road to and from Damascus and Asia. The tolls or duties levied at Capernaum may have been imposed upon the fish and other commerce of the Sea of Galilee, but certainly upon the caravans of merchandise passing to and from Galilee and Judæa.

83. It was from a fishing-boat anchored close to the beach at Capernaum our Lord taught the multitude "in parables," and spake those of the Sower, the Seed, the Harvest and the Reapers, recorded in the fourth chapter of Mark.

84. It was while crossing the lake with His disciples to the eastern side, after teaching the multitude on the shore at Capernaum, a great storm arose endangering the safety of the little ship and all on board. Christ was at the time asleep in the stern. Roused by the cries of the disciples, "He awoke, and rebuked the wind, and said unto the sea, Peace be still. And the wind ceased, and there was a great calm (Mark iv. 39).

85. CAPERNAUM was the city of the evangelist Matthew, who was at first called Levi, son of Alphæus. The New Testament says he sat at the "receipt of custom" when

called by our Lord, which probably means he was a collector of taxes or tolls for the Romans (Matt. ix. 9).

86. It is reasonable to suppose that when Matthew answered the call of Jesus and became one of His personal associates, there was a great religious awakening among the lower and outcast classes in Capernaum. If a "publican" could enter the kingdom of heaven, then there was hope for all men, however humble, obscure, or even degraded (Matt. x. 3).

87. Capernaum was, for a long time, the residence of the Apostle Peter, to which place he removed from Bethsaida. Some think he lived in the house of his wife's mother, whom the Lord healed of a fever (Matt. viii. 14).

88. Capernaum was for some years the residence of Mary, the mother of our Lord. She may have lived there about a year after the first miracle at Cana, and during the first part of Christ's ministry, probably with her sister and her sister's children.

89. The people of Capernaum saw many of the mighty works and heard many of the discourses of our Lord, and yet there were not many that believed on Him. Hence the severe condemnation which He uttered upon the city, saying that though it had been exalted to heaven it should be cast down to hell (Matt. xi. 23).

90. At Capernaum Christ wrought the miracles on the Centurion's servant (Matt. viii. 5); on Simon Peter's mother-in-law (Matt. viii. 14); on the paralytic (Matt. ix. 2); on the man possessed by an unclean spirit; on the daughter of Jairus (Mark v. 22); and on the woman who had an issue of blood (Mark v. 25). There, also, He healed the son of a nobleman by words spoken at Cana several miles away (John iv. 46).

91. At Capernaum our Lord taught His disciples humility by the incident of the little child (Mark ix. 36), and in the synagogue of that city He spake the wonderful discourse recorded in the sixth chapter of John.

92. The doom which our Lord pronounced upon Capernaum and the other unbelieving cities of the Plain of Gennesaret has been remarkably fulfilled. Explorers differ in

their opinion as to the exact site of Capernaum; but be it where it may in the few miles of sea-coast country where it must have stood, only a few ruins tell of the once populous and wealthy city.

93. MEJDEL, a wretched hamlet of twenty huts, a few miles north of Tiberias, and the only inhabited spot on the Plain of Gennesaret, is supposed to be the site of Magdala, the city of Mary Magdalene, out of whom Christ cast seven devils, and to whom He appeared after the Resurrection (Mark xvi. 9; John xx. 2).

94. Near MAGDALA, a little south of it, is a valley with a few cornfields straggling among the ruins of a village and some remains of large buildings with several copious fountains. This is supposed to be DALMANUTHA to "the parts" of which the evangelist Mark says our Lord came in a boat with the disciples after a second time feeding a multitude on the eastern side of the Sea of Galilee (Mark viii. 10).

95. While going towards Magdala from Tiberias, probably where the white cliffs of Dalmanutha came down to the shore, Dr. Tristram saw how the natives now fish in the lake. "An old Arab sat on a low cliff," he writes, "and threw poisoned crumbs of bread as far as he could reach, which the fish seized, and turning over dead were washed ashore and collected for the market. The shoals were marvellous. . . . . No wonder that any net should break which enclosed such a shoal."

96. TIBERIAS is said to occupy the site of RAQQATH, the ancient city of Naphtali; and as the word *raqqath* probably means strip or ribbon of coast, this may be, for the coast is here a long narrow strip between the hills and the Sea of Galilee.

97. King Herod Antipas built Tiberias and called it after his patron, the Emperor Tiberius. Ruins still indicate a city-wall three miles long. Tiberias was completed before our Lord's ministry began.

98. It seems probable that Herod Antipas selected the site of Tiberias because a high hill towered above it on on which he built a castle, and the spot was convenient for

baths, temples, a hippodrome, or circus, and the various needs of a sea-side city. It had in it a great synagogue.

99. From Tiberias, doubtless, came some of the boats which conveyed the people, who eagerly followed Jesus to the distriet on the north-eastern side of the lake (John vi. 2), where was the grassy place on which the five thousand were fed from "five barley loaves and two small fishes," which a lad had brought there in a basket (John vi. 9). The boats probably plied for hire. It is not recorded that Jesus ever visited Tiberias.

100. At Tiberias the water of the Sea of Galilee is not only drinkable but pleasant to the taste. If suspended in porous jars, where there is a current of cool air, it will remain wholesome for some time without losing its agreeable quality.

101. The climate of Tiberias is certainly hot but not specially unhealthy. As a sea-side resort the town and neighbourhood have many attractions; the chief drawback is its filthy condition.

102. There are still some fishermen at Tiberias who, with their boats and nets, recall the trade of Andrew, Peter, John, and James. In the town are three public bath-houses, two old ones, and a modern one; there are also a few private baths and rooms for visitors.

103. The population of Tiberias is now about 6,000, of whom 5,000 are Jews. Of the Christian inhabitants the majority are Greek Catholics.

104. Tiberias was the only defensible city on the western side of the Sea of Galilee. Being close to the sea, and on a hill, it became the seat of government of the Province.

105. The Bay of Et-Tabigah, between Magdala and Capernaum, was one of the best bathing-places on the Lake.

106. On the beach of the Bay of Et Tabigah our Lord must often have walked and taught; and there, too, He may have wrought some of His mighty works.

107. At Et Tabigah are several fountains, and the great Spring which is doubtless the Fountain of Capernaum mentioned by Josephus as watering the Plain of Gennesaret.

108. CHORAZIN, one of the Lake cities in which our Lord did mighty works, could not be far from Capernaum; it might have been at KHERSA on the eastern shore but more probably at KERASEH, northward from Tel Hûm where there are some ruins.

109. BETHSAIDA, which means Fisher-Home, the native place of Andrew, Peter, and Philip (John i. 44), was the name of a village on the eastern bank of the Jordan, and near the river's entrance into the Lake; the tetrarch Philip rebuilt it and re-named it Julias, in honour of the daughter of the Emperor Augustus.

110. Some think there were two Bethsaidas, because John, in his Gospel, speaks of "Bethsaida in Galilee" (John xii. 21); "but this need not mean that it lay west of the Jordan, for the province of Galilee ran right round the Lake, and included most of the level coast-land on the east. The best authorities conclude that there was only one Bethsaida."

111. It was to Bethsaida Julias Jesus withdrew on learning that Herod had beheaded John the Baptist (Luke ix. 10). Not far from Bethsaida was the mountain plateau—"the level plain on the east of the Jordan,"—now known as the Plain of Butaiha where He fed the five thousand. The Plain of Butaiha is very fertile, a fact which helps us to understand the words of the evangelist, "Now there was much grass in the place" (John vi. 10).

112. After the miracle of feeding the 5,000, on the north-eastern shore of the Sea of Galilee, Jesus quitted the disciples and took His way towards Bethsaida by land. Thinking to intercept Him there, the disciples took ship and steered for the place. As they sailed, a storm overtook them, in the midst of which they observed Him walking towards them on the sea. Seeing the Lord, Peter got over the side of the ship and tried to reach Him by walking on the water, and would have been drowned had Jesus not rescued him (Matt. xiv. 30). Mark says, "And He went up into the ship and the wind ceased" (Mark vi. 51). John adds, "And immediately the ship was at the land whither they were going" (John vi. 21).

C

113. The industries of the people who lived around the Sea of Galilee were agriculture, fruit-growing, dyeing, tanning, fishing, fish-curing, and boat-building.

114. The trades of fishing and fish-curing were followed by thousands of Galilean families. The fishing was no monopoly; the fishing grounds, best at the north end of the lake, being free to all, and the trade very profitable.

115. It is supposed that TARICHEÆ stood on the little peninsula of Kerak, lying just where the Jordan flows out of the sea; and that it was of equal importance with Tiberias. Here are the ruins of what must have been a considerable town.

116. Tarichæ is a Greek word, and means "pickling places," and the historian Strabo says that at Tarichæ the Sea of Galilee supplied the best fish for curing.

117. The pickled fish of Galilee were known throughout the Roman world. Not only were large quantities taken up to Jerusalem at the time of the feasts for the multitudes that gathered there, but cargoes of them were carried to the towns of the Mediterranean.

118. The Sea of Galilee attains its greatest width—6¾ miles—at Magdala, opposite which, on the eastern side, is KHERSA, the ancient Gergesa.

119. The meeting of our Lord with the two demoniacs (Matt. viii. 28-34; Mark v. 1-17; Luke viii. 26-36) took place on the eastern shore of the Lake, and a careful examination of the ground shows that there is only one spot where the herd of swine into which the demons entered could have rushed down a steep place into the sea, and that place is Khersa, the ancient Gergesa.

120. The heights of GADARA are to the south of the valley of Yarmuk, and command the plain which looks across the sea towards Tiberias. Here was the city of Gadara, the chief town of the Gadarenes.

121. Describing some glimpses he obtained of the probable appearance of the Lake cities in our Lord's time, Dr. George Adam Smith thus writes, "One of these was at Gadara. Some peasants had just dug up the gravestone of a Roman soldier, whose name was given,—P—— Aelius,

and that he had lived 40 years and served 19; but it also said that he was of a Legion—the Fourteenth. As I read this last detail. . . . I realised how familiar that engine of foreign oppression had been to this region, so that the poor madman could find nothing fitter than it to describe the incubus upon his life. 'My name is Legion,' he said, 'for we are many'" (Mark v. 9).

122. South of Khersa is the GORGE OF FIK, OR APHEK, up which ran the great road of Bethshan, or Scythopolis, to Damascus. The present village of Fik is believed to stand on the site of the ancient Aphek.

INLAND SITES AND TOWNS OF GALILEE.

123. The level tract beyond Magdala is the "**Land of Gennesaret**" (Matt. xiv. 34; Mark vi. 53); the meaning of the name Gennesaret is supposed to have been either Valley of Flowers, or Garden of the Prince. It is about three miles long and one mile broad.

124. The soil of Gennesaret is extremely fertile, and although much of it is over-run with weeds, the cultivated portions supply the markets of Beirout and Damascus with the best melons and cucumbers grown in Palestine.

125. From Tel Hûm, westward, a journey of three hours brings you to SAFED, one of the four holy cities of Palestine of which the Jews say that if prayer should cease to be offered in them, the world would instantly come to an end. The other three holy cities are Jerusalem, Hebron, and Tiberias.

126. Safed, from its situation, is supposed to be "the city set on a hill, which cannot be hid" (Matt. v. 14), mentioned by our Lord in His Sermon on the Mount. But there is no evidence that there was any city on the hill where Safed stands in our Lord's time.

127. The Turkish governor of the district had his quarters at Safed in 1837, when occurred the terrible earthquake which literally shook the town to pieces, and did enormous injury also to Tiberias.

128. Describing the effects of the earthquake of 1837 at Safed, Dr. Thomson says, "The town was dashed to the ground in half a minute"; and in most painful language he describes the sufferings of the wretched people, four-fifths of whom were buried under the ruins, dead or dying: in one night, 4,000 perished in the catastrophe.

129. Not far from Safed is the village of MEIRON, a celebrated Jewish site. Here was buried the great Rabbi Hillel, the grandfather of Rabbi Gamaliel, at whose feet the Apostle Paul sat.

130. At Meiron are the ruins of a Synagogue. A spring near it is called Deborah's fountain, because a tradition says she bathed here on the morning of the murder of Sisera.

131. Two hours' distant from Meiron, near Safed, is KEFR BIRIM, the supposed burial place of Barak, Obadiah, Queen Esther, and others. Here, too, are ruins of a Synagogue.

132. A short distance inland, north-west of Tiberias, is a low hill having two peaks. These two peaks or horns have given it the name of KURUN, or KURN HATTIN, the hill or mountain of the horns; and it is perhaps the most interesting elevation mentioned in the New Testament.

133. The situation and shape of Kurn Hattin so strikingly coincide with the intimations of the Gospel narrative as to leave scarcely a doubt that it is the "Mountain of the Beatitudes," on which our Lord delivered His immortal Sermon on the Mount.

134. The plain on which Kurn Hattin stands is easily accessible from the Lake, or Sea of Galilee; and from the plain to the summit is only a few minutes' walk.

135. The plateau at the summit of Kurn Hattin is well adapted to hold a multitude of people, and it corresponds precisely to the level place, spoken of by Luke, to which our Lord would come down from one of the horns or peaks to address the people.

136. The situation of Kurn Hattin, both to the peasants of the Galilean hills and the fishermen of the Galilean Lake, is such that it would be a natural resort for Jesus and His disciples when they retired for solitude from the towns on

the sea shore, and also for the crowds who came there "from Galilee, from Decapolis, from Jerusalem, from Judæa, and from beyond Jordan."

137. It was on and around Kurn Hattin that in July, 1187, the great Saracen leader, Saladin, finally defeated the Crusaders in a bloody battle. That day saw the triumph of the Muslim, and the complete destruction of the power of the Crusaders in Palestine.

138. A short journey west of Kurn Hattin is KEFR KENNA, now an insignificant village with about 500 inhabitants. For centuries it has been supposed to be the Cana of Galilee where our Lord performed His first miracle at the marriage feast (John ii. 11), where He spake the words which healed the nobleman's son who lay sick at Capernaum several miles distant (John iv. 46), and where Nathanael "the Israelite in whom was no guile" was born (John i. 47).

139. Some eminent Christian travellers, of whom are Drs. Robinson and Porter, have placed Cana of Galilee not at KEFR KENNA, but at KANA-EL-JELIL, near Sepphoris, about nine miles north of Nazareth.

140. At Kefr Kenna is a Greek church where, as at many other churches in Europe and the East, is shewn one of the waterpots said to have been used at the Marriage Feast, at which our Lord turned water into wine.

141. NAZARETH OF GALILEE, fifteen miles west and south of Tiberias, is situated among the hills which form the south ridges of Lebanon, where they begin to sink into the Plain of Jezreel.

142. Among the southern ridges of Lebanon is a valley which runs in a waving line nearly east and west, about a mile long and a quarter of a mile broad, and at a certain point enlarges so as to form a sort of basin. In this basin lies the quiet little town in which the SAVIOUR of men spent His boyhood and much of His life on earth.

143. Of the identification of the ancient site of Nazareth there can be no doubt. The Arab name of the town, which is little larger than an English village, is en-Nazirah, as it was of old.

144. As the traveller approaches the basin or hollow in which Nazareth stands he sees rows of straggling houses rising row over row up a steep slope; nearest to him is a fine large building, a minaret rising a little to the rear. Fig trees, single and in clumps, grow here and there in the valley. Above the town are hills, steep and high, with thin pasture; sheets of rock, fig trees, and now and then an enclosed spot. Such was Nazareth in the time of our Lord.

145. Nazareth is not named in the Old Testament. Its history dates from the time when Mary and Joseph went there to reside with the child Jesus; hence the name by which our Lord was best known among the Jews and the other inhabitants of Palestine—Jesus of Nazareth.

146. With Jerusalem and Bethlehem, Nazareth shares the honour of being the best known and most revered town in the Holy Land.

147. The population of Nazareth is about 5,000. The streets are not more than 6ft. to 10ft. broad, cause-wayed but rough, and having a gutter in the centre. Many of the present houses are new, and give to the little town a bright look seldom seen away from Bethlehem.

148. Nazareth is three days' journey from Jerusalem; about 20 miles from the coast of the Mediterranean; 18 miles from the shore of the Sea of Galilee, and about six miles from Cana and Nain.

149. The people of Nazareth are honourably known for their kindness and courtesy; they are a better class than is to be met with in any other town of Palestine; their habits are more respectable and their dwellings cleaner.

150. Nazareth was the residence of Joseph and Mary, and the place of the Annunciation; for to Nazareth the Angel Gabriel was sent by God "to a virgin espoused to a man whose name was Joseph" (Luke i. 27).

151. It was from Nazareth Joseph and Mary went to Bethlehem very shortly before the birth of Jesus, "to be taxed" (Luke ii. 5), which meant to be counted in the census then being taken in every part of the Roman Empire.

152. After the return from Egypt, Nazareth was the residence of our Lord until He entered upon His public

ministry, "that it might be fulfilled which was spoken by the prophet—He shall be called a Nazarene" (Matt. ii. 23).

153. Now, as in our Lord's time, the title "Nazarene," is a term of contempt. The boys of Nablus greet the Christian traveller or tourist with cries of "Nozrani!" "Nazarene!"

154. Before entering upon His public ministry "Jesus came from Nazareth of Galilee, and was baptized of John in Jordan" (Mark i. 9). Afterwards "He came to Nazareth where He had been brought up" (Luke iv. 16).

155. Coming to Nazareth, after entering upon His public ministry, Jesus preached in the Synagogue, and so offended the townspeople that they rose up and thrust Him out, and led Him unto the brow of the hill whereon the city was built, that they might cast Him down headlong. But He, "passing through the midst of them, went His way and came down to Capernaum" (Luke iv. 16-30).

156. Amongst the sacred places and sites in Nazareth now shewn to travellers are the alleged home of Joseph and Mary; the workshop of Joseph in the Muslim quarter of the town; and the spot where the angel Gabriel appeared to Mary, in the Chapel of the Annunciation, where also stands a marble altar with an inscription in Latin which, translated, reads—"Here the Word was made flesh."

157. Tradition places the Mount of Precipitation, the hill from which the Nazarenes intended to cast Jesus headlong, (Luke iv. 29), about two miles from Nazareth. But intelligent travellers consider it to be a very improbable site; half-a-dozen such hills may be found nearer the town answering all the requirements of the Gospel narrative.

158. There is one sacred spot at Nazareth which need not be questioned; it is the Fountain of the Virgin, described as "a plentiful spring of water issuing from three mouths." To this Fountain women still come, mothers and maidens, to fill their pitchers and carry them away on their heads as their custom is. No one can doubt that Mary often came to this Fountain, carrying the infant Saviour in just the same way mothers of Nazareth carry their children to-day. Probably, too, Jesus often quenched His thirst with water from this "holy well."

159. Not far south of Nazareth is NAIN, a village well and even beautifully situated; like most well-known Palestine villages it has many ruins and rubbish heaps.

160. A supreme interest attaches to Nain, for here our Lord wrought the miracle of restoring to life the son of a widow of the place (Luke vii. 11-18).

161. Seven miles south-east of Nazareth stands MOUNT TABOR; it is one of the most striking objects in southern Galilee. It was here that Deborah commanded Barak to gather his army against Sisera; and "Barak went down from Mount Tabor, and 10,000 men after him. And the Lord discomfited Sisera and all his chariots, and all his host, with the edge of the sword before Barak" (Judges iv. 14-15).

162. Mount Tabor is covered with oak-scrub and other trees of stunted growth, which almost disappear near and at the summit. The western-slope of the mountain is more barren even than the northern; the prevailing bush being the "Christ-thorn" which grows on the limestone of which Tabor consists.

163. From the heights of Tabor grand views are obtained. On the south is the Plain of Jezreel; on the north Endor and its caves; on the east the hills that border the western shore of the Sea of Galilee; on the north-east the Mediterranean.

164. Tabor is mentioned in the Psalms as inspiring the poet with a joyful song of praise (Psalms lxxxix. 12); and Jeremiah, announcing the glory and might of the conqueror of Egypt, exclaims, "As I live, saith the Lord of Hosts, surely as Tabor is among the mountains, and as Carmel by the sea, so shall he come" (Jeremiah xlvi. 18).

165. The possession of Mount Tabor was always deemed of first-rate importance by the leaders of armies in the wars with which Palestine was so often visited. This mountain and its immediate neighbourhood have been inhabited from very early times.

166. ENDOR is a village two or three miles south-east of Nain, supposed to be the scene of the deaths of Jabin and Sisera (Judges iv.), and still famous for its caves.

167. In one of the caves of Endor Saul sought a Witch on the night before the disastrous battle of Gilboa. (1 Sam. xxviii. 7). By her incantations he hoped to bring again from the other world the prophet Samuel. To the surprise and terror both of the Witch and Saul the prophet appeared, and pronounced the death sentence of the proud and reckless king.

168. A little to the south of Nain is SHUNEM, now called Sûlem, a village which is a great contrast in tidiness and cleanliness to many villages now to be seen in Palestine.

169. At Shunem the Philistines had their encampment during the war against Saul.

170. It was a woman of Shunem who showed hospitality to the prophet Elisha. Seeing that he was a "man of God," she said to her husband, "Let us make a little chamber, I pray thee, on the wall, and let us set for him there a bed, a table, and a stool, and a lamp, and it shall be when he cometh to us he shall turn in thither" (2 Kings iv. 10). And so the prophet did.

171. Elisha paid a second visit to Shunem when, entreated by the woman who had there given him hospitality years before, he returned from his abode on Mount Carmel and restored her dead son to life (2 Kings iv. 18-37).

172. Jerome refers to the hill on which Shunem lies as LITTLE HERMON; it is probably the "HILL OF MOREH" where the Midianites and Amalekites were encamped when attacked and routed by Gideon and his three hundred picked men (Judges vii.).

173. Shunem is now a hamlet of a few mud huts, with a garden of lemon trees inside a cactus-hedge, a fountain and trough.

174. BETHSHAN, or Beth-Shean, now called BEISAN, although once a famous Old Testament site, is now a miserable village of about sixty mud huts, with a marshy rivulet making its slow way through the place.

175. Ancient BETHSHAN, also called SCYTHOPOLIS, was a city of not less than two or three miles in circumference; on the site are ruins of a temple, of an amphitheatre, and of a long thick city wall.

176. On the walls of Bethshan the bodies of Saul and Jonathan were hung up by the Philistines after the battle of Gilboa. It was a bold deed of the men of Jabesh to go there by night and carry them away to bury them with fitting tokens of respect under a tamarisk tree in their own place (1 Samuel xxxi. 10-13).

177. In our Lord's time the district of Bethshan was called also "BETHANIA," meaning "soft soil"; hence the later name of Bethany, a name given to BETHABARA, the crossing place of the Jordan in Bethshan, where John the Baptist baptized.

178. Although the famous AIN-HAROD, "the Spring of Trembling" (Judges vii.), at which Gideon tested the quality of his soldiers by the way in which they drank of its waters, is by some identified with the "Fountain of Jezreel," near Zerin, Major Conder is in favour of the "Fountain of the Two Troops," a large spring not far west of the Gilboan hills, where they bend to the south.

179. SEPPHORIS, the ancient Sefuriah, a city standing on a hill midway between and a little to the west of Nazareth and Cana, was the capital of Galilee before Herod Antipas transferred that honour to his newly-built city, Tiberias.

180. In the time of Josephus, Sepphoris was the largest town in Galilee, and after the destruction of Jerusalem till the fourth century it was one of the head-quarters of the Jewish people. The Sanhedrin sometimes held its sittings there.

181. EL-JISH, a village three miles north of Meiron, once called GISCALA, may be mentioned as having been the residence of the ancestors of the Apostle Paul before they migrated to Tarshish.

182. Like Meiron, GISCALA is in a poor farming country, where the people may be seen riding on asses without saddle or bridle in a humble way. She asses are preferred as being easier in their step. Now and then a foal runs by its mother's side, recalling the words of Zechariah, "Shout, O daughter of Jerusalem, behold thy King cometh unto thee; He is just and having salvation; lowly, and riding upon an ass, and upon a colt, the foal of an ass" (Zechariah ix. 9).

183. Lake Huleh, also called the "Waters of Merom," is a sheet of water four miles long and two miles broad, and about nine miles north of the Sea of Galilee.

184. The country around Lake Merom and the northern portion of the River Jordan is the haunt of innumerable water-fowl; the reedy borders of the lake and the river are the lairs of swine and other wild beasts.

185. It was to the country around Lake Merom that Herod the Great, physically a strong man and fond of outdoor exercise, came to hunt the game which then literally swarmed there.

186. Near Lake Merom was fought the great battle between the Israelites and the Canaanites which gave Northern Palestine into the hands of Joshua.

187. Four miles north-west of Lake Merom are the ruins of KADESH, on a hill over-looking a fine plain bearing the same name. Barak was a native of Kadesh (Judges iv. 6).

188. The present village of EL-HARATHIYEH, near Mount Carmel, is the ancient "HAROSHETH OF THE GENTILES" (Judges iv. 13), where Sisera lived. An enormous double mound may mark the castle of Sisera, the watch-tower of the Gentiles who then lorded it over Israel.

189. BEIROUT is the most important sea-port of Northern Palestine. It has a large trade in silk; plantations of mulberries and the skilful cultivation of the silk-worm are chief features in the occupations of the people.

190. At Beirout, as at other towns, Herod Agrippa, besides building baths and theatres sought to please the populace by fights in the circus in which gladiators contended with one another, or with wild beasts.

191. At Beirout and at Cæsarea Philippi Titus made bands of Jewish prisoners, taken at the siege and fall of Jerusalem, engage in mortal strife with each other, to enliven the holidays.

SAMARIA.

192. **Samaria**, the name of the province of Palestine which lies between Galilee and Judæa, was at first restricted to the city built by Omri, King of Israel, which became the capital of the kingdom of the ten tribes until the captivity.

193. The name, SAMARIA, is derived from Shemer, the name of the man from whom the hill on which the city was built was first purchased.

194. The city of Samaria was for a long time a centre of idol-worship. Here Ahab built the Temple of Baal, which was destroyed by Jehu. "Ahab made a grove," and "Ahab did more to provoke the Lord God of Israel than all the Kings of Israel that were before him" (1 Kings xvi. 32-33).

195. Samaria was besieged by the Syrians during the reign of Ahab, but Ben-hadad, of Damascus, the Syrian general, was defeated by a small force of Israelites (2 Kings vi. 24). After several sieges, the place fell into the hands of the Romans. Pompey restored it to Syria; then Augustus gave it to Herod the Great, who rebuilt and adorned it and called it Sebaste.

196. Samaria is now a small, dirty village surrounded by hedges of cactus, containing ruins which, even out of its present desolation, speak of its former grandeur.

197. Dr. Thomson says of Samaria, "The remains of the ancient city consist mainly of colonnades which certainly date back to the time of the Herods. . . . The grand colonnade runs along the south side of the hill down a broad terrace. . . . The number of columns, whole or broken along this line, is nearly one hundred."

198. The terrible scenes of the siege of Samaria as recorded in the Second Book of Kings are recalled by the visitor as he walks amidst the ruins. The compact of the starving women, for example, "Give thy son that we may eat him to-day, and we will eat my son to-morrow" (2 Kings vi. 28); of the four lepers who sat at the city gate, and said one to another, "Why sit we here until we die?" (2 Kings vii. 3) and then, going into the city, found "there was no one in it, for the Syrians had fled."

199. The most interesting sites in Samaria pointed out to travellers are the gate where the lepers sat; the palace of Ahab; the temple built by Herod, and the very picturesque ruin of the Church of St. John erected by the Crusaders.

200. Jerome is responsible for the tradition that John the Baptist was buried in Samaria; a most improbable story seeing that John was beheaded in the Castle of Machærus, near the Dead Sea. Nevertheless is his tomb pointed out there, also the tomb of Obadiah and other famous Scripture characters.

201. SAMARIA, THE PROVINCE, is bounded on the north by Galilee; on the east by the Jordan; on the south by Judæa, and on the west by the Mediterranean Sea.

202. The Province of Samaria may be described as the central highland of Palestine which rises in the north from the Plain of Esdraelon. Small sheltered hollows lie among the hills; the valleys trend gently westward towards the sea; while on the east ravines descend more abruptly into the Jordan valley.

203. The occupations of the Samaritans were almost entirely those connected with farming, cattle-rearing, and fruit-growing.

204. The pastures of the Province of Samaria were exceedingly fertile, providing food for a famous breed of cattle, not to be excelled for the quantity and quality of their milk.

205. Five miles south of the city of Samaria, is the ancient SHECHEM, called in the New Testament Sychem. It is rich in Biblical associations.

206. Shechem is the earliest mentioned town in the Bible; Abraham visited it both as he went down into (Genesis xii. 6) and returned from (Genesis xiii. 3-4) Egypt.

207. In Abraham's time an oak tree grew at or near Shechem, under which he pitched his tent and built an altar; the first Sanctuary of Jehovah in the Land of Promise. On this spot is now the hamlet of BALATA, which in Samaritan means "The Holy Oak."

208. Under the "Holy Oak" of Shechem, Jacob buried the *teraphim*—the little home-gods for which Rachel cared

so much, and the heathen amulets of his household. He, too, like his grandfather, built an altar to Jehovah there (Genesis xxxv. 4).

209. Joshua recognised Shechem as a "holy place" long after the patriarchs were dead, for he set up a great stone under the oak that was by the Sanctuary of God, as a witness that it had "heard all the words of the Lord which He spake" (Joshua xxiv. 26-27).

210. Near to Shechem is *Jacob's Well*, the authenticity of which has never been doubted. To-day, as in every past epoch, the Jews can say, "Our father Jacob gave us this well."

211. Jacob's Well is to all Christian people the most "sacred place" in Palestine and, indeed, in the world, because only there, within a space of a few square yards, is it possible to say our Lord and Saviour stood or sat. No such certainty attaches to any other spot (John iv. 6).

212. While seated upon the margin of Jacob's Well, our Lord held the memorable conversation with a woman of Samaria, recorded in the fourth chapter of John's Gospel. The woman came from SYCHAR, a village now called "Askar," lying at the foot of Mount Ebal.

213. According to Dr. Geikie, Jacob's Well "is cut through a thick bed of soil swept down in the course of the ages by the rains from the hills on each side; and beneath this deposit it passes through soft rock, the water filtering in through the sides, to the depth occasionally of about 12 feet, even yet, though it is now dry in summer, and sometimes for years together."

214. The mouth and upper part of Jacob's Well are lined with stone. Over the Well is a stone slab with a round hole in the middle, large enough for the skin-buckets of the peasants to pass through. A Greek church is now in course of erection over the Well.

215. That Jacob's Well is sometimes dry for years together is proved by this incident: over 40 years ago a boy allowed himself to be let down for the purpose of finding and bringing up a Bible dropped into the well accidentally three years

before, and, strange to say, he found it, the bottom being quite dry at the time.

216. "Looking from Mount Ebal over the scene below, the traveller sees, at the mouth of a glen, a little heap of stones. The road comes up to it by which the patriarchs first entered the land. This little heap lies over JACOB'S WELL. To-day the shadow of a telegraph post falls upon it."

217. The VALLEY OF SHECHEM is one of the most beautiful localities in Palestine. Wood, water, and mountain, and even the singing of birds, combine to make it delightful. At its widest part it is half-a-mile, but for the most part it is about a furlong in width.

218. The Valley of Shechem is a natural amphitheatre formed by the receding of Mounts Gerizim and Ebal at the same point, and is wonderfully suited to such an incident as that of the reading of the law to the Hebrews, at the great assembly of the nation after the taking of Ai by Joshua.

219. The site of ancient Shechem is now occupied by NABLUS, a contraction of the Roman name, Neapolis, which means "the new city."

220. NABLUS lies between the two famous mountains, Gerizim and Ebal; Gerizim rising on the south in bold, angular masses of rock; Ebal rising on the north, with its many terraces of prickly pear.

221. It was on the lower parts of GERIZIM and EBAL, and in the valley between, that Joshua assembled the tribes of Israel after they had entered the Promised Land. "And all Israel, and their elders, and officers, and their judges, stood on this side the ark and on that side . . . half of them over against Mount Gerizim, and half of them over against Mount Ebal; as Moses, the servant of the Lord, had commanded before, that they should bless the people of Israel. And afterward Joshua read all the words of the law, the blessings and cursings, according to all that is written in the book of the law" (Joshua viii. 33, 34).

222. The height of MOUNT GERIZIM is 2,849 feet; of MOUNT EBAL 3,077 feet. The tops of the two mountains are two miles apart.

223. On a plateau of Mount Gerizim the Samaritans encamp for the celebration of the Feast of the Passover, which they continue to observe with all the ancient rites and customs and much more than the ancient ceremonial display.

224. On the top of Gerizim are the ruins of a castle and the sculptured stones of some earlier building. Near to the castle are some massive stones which legend identifies with the twelve stones brought up from Jordan and set up at Gilgal as a memorial.

225. Claiming to be the real Israel of God the Samaritans regard the higher plateau on Gerizim as their sacred place. Towards it they turn in prayer, and they never approach it but with uncovered feet.

226. On the higher plateau of Gerizim, say the Samaritans, Abraham offered up Isaac, and Jacob had the vision of the heavenly ladder. These and other statements they make in opposition to the statements of the Judæan Jews.

227. A few of the descendants of the ancient Samaritan people still live in NABLUS; they number about 150. They have a high priest, and support a Synagogue, where are kept three manuscripts of the Pentateuch, two of which are of considerable antiquity, but the third is of a very great age. Each is written on parchment and folded upon a roll having an embossed cover.

228. Many villages and remains of villages still dot the lower slopes of Ebal and Gerizim. It is allowable to think that the inhabitants of even a much greater number of villages in that district saw Jesus and heard Him speak during His stay amongst the Samaritans.

229. A little way from Shechem is the TOMB OF JOSEPH (Joshua xxiv. 32), in outward appearance an ordinary Syrian tomb in an open-air enclosure beside a little ruined mosque.

230. Both Jews and Samaritans offer burnt offerings at the tomb of Joseph. These offerings no longer consist of animals, but of fabrics such as shawls and silks for garments.

231. The peculiar feature of Joseph's tomb consists in two pedestals with shallow cups on their tops, placed one at

the head, the other at the foot of the grave; these serve the pious visitors for altars.

232. South of Shechem is SHILOH where Joshua divided the land among the tribes, and the Tabernacle was reared (Joshua xviii. 1).

233. At Shiloh Eli dwelt, the high-priest of the Tabernacle; and thither Hannah, the mother of Samuel, came yearly, bringing with her the "little coat" which her boy wore as Eli's attendant (1 Samuel ii. 19).

234. Where ancient Shiloh stood is now a heap of ruins, a graphic fulfilment of the destruction which Jeremiah said had fallen upon the place because of the wickedness of the people (Jeremiah vii. 12).

235. South-west of Shiloh is BETHEL, originally called Luz (Genesis xxviii. 19); it is in the very heart of Palestine.

236. To Bethel, then called Luz, Abraham came and raised there an altar, calling upon the name of the Lord, Who had given the land to him and to his posterity (Genesis xii. 8).

237. LUZ was the "certain place" to which Jacob came when he journeyed from Beersheba to Haran. It being late when he arrived, he tarried there all night; "And he took one of the stones of the place and put it under his head and lay down to sleep. And he dreamed, and behold a ladder set up on the earth, and the top of it reached to heaven; and behold the angels of God ascending and descending on it" (Genesis xxviii. 11-12).

238. When Jacob had dreamed of the mystic ladder at Luz, and of receiving a renewal of the blessing promised to Abraham and to Isaac, he awoke, set up a stone pillar as a memorial, poured oil upon it, and changed the name of the place to Bethel, the "House of God" (Genesis xxviii. 19).

239. At or near Bethel the prophet Elisha was mocked and jeered at by a number of children, forty-two of whom were torn by two she-bears that issued from an adjoining wood (2 Kings ii. 23-24).

240. Once the most sacred place in Palestine to the Israelites, Bethel became the centre of idolatrous worship, and its name was changed to Beth-haven, "the house of

idols." Like Shiloh it was cursed, and "came to nought," as the ruins which now cover its site bear witness.

241. A short distance eastward from Bethel was AI, which means "The Heap"; it is now called "El Tel"—the Mound or Heap.

242. A few miles south of Bethel is GIBEAH (1 Samuel x. 26), where Saul, Israel's peasant King, lived, and where, sitting by the wall of his rude palace, he held a feast every new moon with his favourite companions in arms (1 Samuel xx. 5).

243. It was at Gibeah David gave up to the Gibeonites the two sons of Rizpah, together with five sons of Saul's daughter, Michal, to be put to death. Rizpah's agony for the loss of her sons, and her heroic protection of their dead bodies from the wild beasts and the birds of prey, form one of the most pathetic stories in the Old Testament (2 Samuel xxi. 6-11).

244. Half-an-hour's journey south of Bethel is EL-BIREH, the ancient BEEROTH, a name meaning "Wells." Beeroth was the birth-place of one of David's mighty men, Naharai, the Beerothite.

245. Beeroth has about 800 inhabitants, an excellent spring of water, ruins of reservoirs, and an old Khan.

246. Beeroth stands on a high hill, 2,800 feet above the level of the sea, and commands a splendid prospect. A strong and prosperous place in the time of the Crusaders, it is now miserable enough.

247. Tradition has fixed upon Beeroth as the first halting-place of Joseph and Mary on that memorable journey from Jerusalem to Nazareth, when, the day after leaving the Holy City, they discovered that Jesus was not with them (Luke ii. 45).

248. In the centre of Samaria and of its most truly classic district is RAMAH, identified with El-Ram, once a strong fortress, now a wretched village, the mingled hovels and ruins of which tell of a glory long departed.

249. It was at Ramah, in Benjamin, the Chaldeans collected their prisoners of war before marching them off to Babylon, a circumstance alluded to by Jeremiah when he

imagined the spirit of Rachel, the mother of the tribe, to have left her tomb by the wayside, near Bethlehem, to grieve over the many that would never return. "A voice was heard in Ramah, lamentation and bitter weeping; Rachel weeping for her children, refused to be comforted, because they were not" (Jeremiah xxxi. 15).

250. It was while journeying through Samaria to Jerusalem that the inhabitants of a Samaritan village refused to give hospitality to our Lord and His disciples; and John and James, indignant, inquired of Him, "Wilt Thou that we bid fire to come down from heaven and consume them? But He turned, and rebuked them" (Luke ix. 54).

251. Although our Lord, early in His ministry, forbade the disciples to "go into any city of the Samaritans" (Matt. x. 5-6) but first to "go to the lost sheep of the house of Israel," He subsequently visited the Samaritans without hesitation or reserve; and, after the Resurrection, the Apostles preached the Gospel in Samaria with much success.

252. The hatred of the Jews against the Samaritans is forcibly illustrated by John in the 8th chapter of his Gospel, where he reports that the Jews, angry with Jesus, called Him a Samaritan, and said scornfully to Him, "Thou hast a devil."

253. Many of the Christians of Jerusalem fled to the "region" of Samaria during the first persecution which arose there, and in which Saul, afterwards Paul, took a leading part, "laying waste the Church" (Acts viii. 1-3).

254. It was to the city of Samaria that Philip, as the Acts of the Apostles records, came preaching the Gospel, and with such success that "the people with one accord gave heed unto those things which Philip spake, hearing him, and seeing the miracles which he did. And there was great joy in that city" (Acts viii. 5-6).

255. It was by the preaching of Philip that a famous magician, named Simon, who "bewitched the people of Samaria," was converted and "continued with Philip; and beholding signs and great miracles wrought, he was amazed" (Acts viii. 9-13).

256. Hearing of the success of Philip's preaching in Samaria the Apostles in Jerusalem sent Peter and John to help to carry on the good work (Acts viii. 14); which they did, preaching the Gospel "to many villages of the Samaritans" (Acts viii. 25).

257. In one of the Lord's most beautiful parables, if indeed it be a parable and not the narrative of a real incident, "a good Samaritan" is selected to contrast with a bigoted priest and a cold-hearted Levite (Luke x. 33).

258. The most charming scenery in Samaria was at and around Shechem. "The land of Syria," said Mahomet, "is beloved by Allah beyond all lands, and the part of Syria which He loveth most is the district of Jerusalem, and the place which He loveth most in the district of Jerusalem is the mountain of Nablus."

259. Of the mountains of Samaria, not the least impressive, and certainly the most famous after Ebal and Gerizim, is MOUNT CARMEL, frequently called Mar Elyas, from its association with the great prophet Elijah.

260. MOUNT CARMEL forms one of the most striking and characteristic features of Palestine; it is a noble ridge, projecting into the Mediterranean.

261. Mount Carmel forms the southern boundary of the Bay of Acre, from which it extends about twelve miles inland, running to the south-east and terminating in a bold cliff overlooking the low hills of Samaria.

262. The ridge of Carmel forms a great natural wall between the sea-washed Plain of Sharon on the south and the inland Plain of Esdraelon on the north. Its highest point is 1,600 feet above the level of the sea.

263. The word Carmel means "the well-wooded place," or "the Park," and in appearance Mount Carmel still justifies its name.

264. Travellers delight to describe the rocky dells of Carmel, with their deep jungles; its "shrubberies thicker than any others in Central Palestine"; its woods of oaks and evergreens full of game and wild animals, and its garden-like spots where grow hollyhocks, jasmine, and many a flowering creeper.

265. On Carmel the roebuck is still hunted; the natives call it the Yahmûr, a name which occurs in the Bible as the Hebrew word for a species of deer.

266. Being regarded as a sacred mountain, in one or more of the caves of which Elijah may have found an occasional abode, many Christian hermits have chosen to live solitary lives in the caves and cells of Mount Carmel.

267. The celebrated Convent on Mount Carmel is said to stand over the cave in which Elijah sought shelter when Ahab was seeking to slay him; but its fame is really due to the barefooted Carmelite Monks that sprung up on Carmel and are known all over the world, and who claim Elijah as their originator and the first member of their brotherhood.

268. Two hours and a half distant from the Carmel Convent is EL MOUHRATTAH, the scene of Elijah's sacrifice. It is a natural terrace, with huge blocks of stone, some of which would make admirable altars.

269. On the eastern end of the ridge of Carmel Elijah recalled Israel to allegiance to Jehovah, and slew the prophets of the false god Baal.

270. On or near the eastern end of Carmel Elijah "caused fire to come down from heaven" to consume the bands of fifties and their captains whom Ahaziah sent to take the prophet prisoner because he stopped the king's messengers to Baal-Zebub, the god of Ekron. A shapeless ruin now marks the spot, bearing an Arab name which means "the burning" (2 Kings i.).

271. It was at some spot on Mount Carmel Elisha received the visit of the bereaved mother of Shunem whose son he soon restored to her alive and well (2 Kings iv. 25).

272. In Hebrew eyes Mount Carmel had a rare sanctity; its richness and impressive scenery inspired more than one great prophet to praise it in song.

273. Only one important sea-port is to be found on the coast of Samaria between Acre and Joppa, namely, the town of CÆSAREA. It is frequently mentioned in the Acts of the Apostles.

274. CÆSAREA having a good harbour was in olden time a convenient and valuable port on the line of route from Tyre to Egypt. It is about 70 miles from Jerusalem.

275. Cæsarea was for several years the residence and sphere of the missionary work of the Evangelist Philip.

276. At Cæsarea dwelt Cornelius, the devout and charitable centurion of "the Italian band;" he and his family were the first Gentile converts made by the Apostle Peter after his vision at Joppa (Acts x.).

277. To Cæsarea came Peter when his prison doors at Jerusalem were miraculously opened for him (Acts xii. 19).

278. From Cæsarea Paul sailed to Tarsus when forced to quit Jerusalem on his return from Damascus after his conversion (Acts ix. 30).

279. It was at Cæsarea Paul landed after his second missionary journey; and, after saluting the Christian brethren of the Church there, "went down to Antioch" (Acts xviii. 22).

280. The Apostle Paul spent some time in Cæsarea on his return from his third missionary journey, and found entertainment in the house of Philip, who "had four daughters, virgins, who did prophecy" (Acts xxi. 8-9).

281. While the guest of Philip, Paul was visited by Agabus, who, taking Paul's girdle, bound the Apostle's hands and feet, saying, "So shall the Jews of Jerusalem bind the man who weareth this girdle, and shall deliver him into the hands of the Gentiles" (Acts xxi. 10-11).

282. Refusing to heed the warning of the prophet Agabus, Paul, with certain of the disciples of Cæsarea, went up to Jerusalem, to be soon brought back a prisoner, remaining two years in the place, in bonds, before his voyage to Rome.

283. It was in Cæsarea Paul had those remarkable interviews with the great rulers of the province during which, as he reasoned of righteousness, temperance, and judgment to come, Felix trembled and Agrippa declared "With but little persuasion thou wouldst fain make me a Christian" (Acts xxvi. 28).

284. Cæsarea was orginally but a small sea-port, but Herod the Great rebuilt, enlarged, and adorned it with much splendour.

285. In its palmy days Cæsarea had an amphitheatre, palaces, baths, and temples; its quays were alive with

commerce, and the legions of Rome often trod its lovely but now almost forsaken shore.

286. Of the four or five streams which flow westward and empty themselves into the Mediterranean Sea between Cæsarea and Joppa, the Zerka or Crocodile River is the largest. They all flow through deep and dangerous marshes; but the Zerka until recent years had another danger, namely, the crocodiles, which lived in it, and lay in its mud and papyrus reeds, as comfortably as in the Nile.

THE PLAIN OF SHARON.

287. The **Plain of Sharon** is really the north-western portion of the Maritime Plain. It extends from the slopes of Carmel southward to Joppa, and from the Mediterranean eastward to the Central Range.

288. Josephus describes the Plain of Sharon as the "place called the Forest"; Strabo called it "a great Forest"; the Crusaders "the Forest of Assur"; Tasso "the enchanted Forest"; and Napoleon "the Forest of Miski," from the present village of Miskieh.

289. The Plain of Sharon has had a just fame for fertility. Up to the time of the Crusaders it was, mainly, a great forest interspersed with clearings or open spaces. Poorly cultivated in the northern portion, it yields generously to good tillage in the south, and the traveller there finds corn-fields, gardens, groves of oranges, melons, and palms. It is not devoid of water, but is best watered in the north.

290. The "Rose of Sharon" mentioned in the Song of Solomon (Song of Solomon ii. 1), was one of the many flowers which still grow on the Plain of Sharon, but which was the real rose it is impossible to decide. Perhaps it was a species of mallow, perhaps narcissus, meadow-saffron, anemone, lily, or asphodel, or perhaps the oleander; all these flowers grow there in profusion in the months of April and May.

291. As the traveller crosses the Plain of Sharon he will see peasants ploughing with the plough in one hand, and in the other a long wooden goad the sharp point of which is used to urge forward the lean, small oxen. It is no use for

them to kick against it. This is the goad alluded to in the words of the Lord Jesus spoken to Saul on his journey to Damascus (Acts ix. 5).

292. Not many cattle are pastured on the Plain of Sharon, but the flocks of sheep are numerous; probably they are of the same broad-tailed breed reared by the ancient Hebrews, for we read that the tail of the animal was burned by the priest on the altar for a thank-offering.

293. According to Major Conder, "scattered oak woods, sandy dunes, marshes, and boggy streams" occupy the greater part of the Plain of Sharon to-day; the same authority describes its present inhabitants as being the most lawless in Palestine.

JUDÆA.

294. **Judæa** is the southernmost Province of Palestine, comprising the original portions of the Promised Land assigned to Judah, Benjamin, Dan, and Simeon; it is almost identical with the ancient kingdom of Judah.

295. The Province of Judæa is bounded on the north by Samaria; on the east by the River Jordan and the Dead Sea; on the south by the Negeb and the Arabian desert; and on the west by the Mediterranean Sea.

296. Generally speaking, Judæa includes the Shephelah, and the Maritime Plain from a point a little north of Joppa; if these be regarded separately, then there is left a piece of territory familiarly known as "the hill-country of Judæa," between which and the Shephelah there is a series of well-defined valleys.

297. Apart from the Shephelah and the Maritime Plain, Judæa is a very small country, being only 55 miles in length, and from 25 to 30 in breadth. Its area is not over 1,400 square miles, of which one half may be called desert.

298. The central portion of Judæa is a table-land from 2,000 to 3,000 feet above the level of the sea, 35 miles in length and from 12 to 17 miles in breadth. This plateau stands out in history as prominently as an island, and it *is* an island, though the sea no longer surrounds it.

299. On the north of Judæa lie the valleys and mountains of Samaria, the last ten miles of the table-land of Judæa being in Benjamin and forming a desolate tract of rocky platforms and ridges, of moorland strewn with boulders, and fields of shallow soil thickly mixed with stone. This wild tract was the site of more fortresses, sieges, battles, forays, and massacres than perhaps any other part of Palestine.

300. On the east of the Judæan plateau is the great land-gulf which lies between it and the Dead Sea. "From the level of the plateau," writes Dr. G. A. Smith, "the land sinks swiftly, and, as it seems, shuddering through softer formations, desert and chaotic, to a depth of which you cannot see the bottom,—but you know that it falls far below the level of the ocean to the coasts of a bitter sea."

301. The Judæan plateau has for its southern boundary the Negeb, across which ran the highway from Bethel, by Hebron, to Beersheba. Branches of this road diverged to Arabia and Egypt. Along one of them Elijah fled from Jezebel, and modern travellers go to Sinai. Along another, leading to Egypt, Abraham must have travelled to and fro; Hagar fled from Sarah, hoping to escape into her own country, and Jacob journeyed to Egypt.

302. On the west, the boundary of Judæa, taken at its widest, was the Mediterranean Sea; but as the Maritime Plain was only at intervals a Jewish possession, and the Shephelah always debatable ground, the true western boundary of Judæa was the series of valleys separating the Shephelah from the Central Range of hills forming the back-bone of Palestine.

303. Judæa was the first home, the stronghold and the sepulchre of God's ancient people—the Hebrews. For Christians it is enough to remember that Judæa contains the places where our Lord Jesus Christ was born, crucified, and buried; the scenes, too, of His agony and the more painful events of His life and ministry.

JOPPA OR JAFFA.

304. **Joppa,** now called **Jaffa,** was in past time, as it is now, the Port of Jerusalem. It is known throughout the civilised world as the port of arrival and departure of tourists in Palestine.

305. Joppa is forty miles from Jerusalem. The route to the Holy City is partly over the Plain of Sharon going either to Ramleh direct, or by Lydda to Ramleh. Between Ramleh and Jerusalem every spot recalls some Bible person, incident, or event.

306. The immemorial methods of journeying from Jaffa to Jerusalem are still in use, namely, on foot, or horse, or camel back; or in a kind of rude carriage. But recently a railway has been constructed between the world-famed city and its port, and passengers may now go by rail.

307. To Joppa is assigned a very remote—even an antediluvian antiquity. On its rocky shore, say some ancient writers, Andromeda was exposed to the sea-monster, and the chains by which she was bound were shown in the time of Pliny, therefore of our Lord also.

308. Joppa was the landing place of the cedar and pinewood sent by sea by Hiram of Tyre to King Solomon for the building of the first "house of habitation" ever made with hands for the invisible Jehovah (2 Chron. ii. 16).

309. It was by way of Joppa that, by permission of King Cyrus, the materials were conveyed from the coasts of Tyre and Sidon to Jerusalem for the re-building of the Second Temple under Zerubbabel (Ezra iii. 7).

310. At Joppa the prophet Jonah took ship "to flee unto Tarshish from the presence of the Lord," and then went through the singular experience of being three days and three nights in the belly of a great fish, which Christ used as typical of His own burial and period of entombment (Jonah i. 3).

311. In the time of the Apostles, a considerable number of Jews dwelt in Joppa (Acts ix. 36); among them was Dorcas, who died "full of good works and alms deeds," and

was raised to life again by the Apostle Peter, who was sent for from Lydda where he was residing at the time.

312. Coming from LYDDA to Joppa at the desire of the Christian converts to restore Dorcas to life, Peter lodged in the house of Simon the tanner, where, in the dream of a "sheet" let down from heaven containing clean and unclean beasts, the Apostle was commanded to regard no human being as unclean, but to include the Gentiles in the fold of Christ (Acts x.).

313. A house in Joppa, said to be the dwelling of Simon the tanner, is still shown to travellers, and the late Dean Stanley considered that the circumstances were all in favour of the site, if not the very house itself, having been truly identified.

314. The name Joppa, or Jaffa, signifies beauty. Built upon a bold, romantic rock, and commanding splendid views on all sides, the name "tower of joy" or beauty, is not inappropriate to it.

315. The beauty of Joppa does not extend to its interior. The houses are built promiscuously; the streets are narrow, dirty, and irregular. Its population approaches 30,000, of which about a thousand are Christians, three thousand are Jews, and the rest Mahometans.

316. Joppa has a valuable trade in fruits. Its oranges are allowed to be the finest in all Palestine; eight millions of them are exported annually, and they are sometimes sold in the streets of the town at the rate of eight or ten a penny.

317. For miles around Joppa are orange groves, gardens, and orchards, making a panorama of luxuriant beauty and filling the air with a delicious aroma.

TOWNS AND SITES ON THE SHEPHELAH.

318. Travelling from Joppa to Lydda, after crossing the broad plain, undulating in low waves towards the hills in the east, "the Shephelah is reached, known in the Bible as the 'Low Lands.'"

319. In the Shephelah, as elsewhere in Palestine, the country well illustrates our Lord's parables, for it is cultivated

in patches, or planted with olives, many of which are among the hills far from the villages. Thus the peasant has still "to go forth to sow," often to a considerable distance from his home (Mark iv. 3).

320. LYDDA is famous as being the reputed birthplace of St. George, the patron saint of England. He is said to have suffered martyrdom in Nicomedia, the capital of ancient Bithynia, from which his remains, it is averred, were carried to Lydda, where his head is still thought to lie below the altar of the church which bears his name.

321. Lydda used to be a thriving place, having large soap works and a good trade. It is now only one of a number of poor villages of mud hovels mingled with ruins.

322. There was a Christian "fellowship" at Lydda very early in Apostolic days. Peter found it there when he went down to the saints that were at Lydda and healed the paralytic Æneas (Acts ix. 32-35).

323. LYDDA and RAMLEH are only two miles apart, each having a belt of verdure round it, contrasting strongly with the desolate treeless country beyond.

324. The dwellings of the peasants at and around Lydda and Ramleh are mud-houses built of bricks made of clay and chopped straw, and sun-dried. Such dwellings need frequent repairs, the rain soon finding its way through the roofs and soaking the walls. Only by constant oversight are they kept water-tight. As in the days of Ecclesiastes: "By slothfulness the roof sinketh in; and through idleness of the hands the house leaketh" (Eccles. x. 18).

325. About two miles west of Ramleh is a small village called RANTIEH, which some think is the site of Arimathea, the birth-place of that devoted follower of our Lord who provided for Him a tomb (Matt. xxvii. 57-60.)

326. Among the hills north-east of Lydda lies TIBNEH, the ancient Timnath-serah (Joshua xxiv. 30), where are many old Jewish tombs, one of which is said to be the burial place of Joshua, the successor of Moses in the leadership of Israel.

327. Six miles east of Lydda, on the top of a hill, are some mud and stone houses, water cisterns, and a few ruins;

this is MODIN, the birth-place of the illustrious brotherhood of the Maccabees.

328. The olive-groves between Lydda and Tibneh are a favourite haunt of the turtle-dove, a bird more numerous in Palestine than anywhere else. The offering of Mary in the Temple, after the birth of our Lord, consisted of turtle-doves or young pigeons; an evidence of her poverty, such birds being the usual offerings of the poor (Luke ii. 24).

329. A Roman road by which possibly the Apostle Paul was taken from Jerusalem to Cæsarea runs through Tibneh. It is so rough and bad as to be distressing to the traveller. "Had we been grandees," writes one of a company who traversed it, "it might have been made better for us; for it is still the custom, as it was in ancient days, to 'prepare the way,' to 'make the crooked straight and the rough places plain' for great people."

THE PHILISTINE AND SAMSON COUNTRY.

330. South of Joppa, along the coast-plain, was the **Country of the Philistines,** whose five chief cities were EKRON, GATH, ASHDOD, ASCALON, and GAZA.

331. The famous cities of the Philistines are now, with the exception of Gaza, no longer important places. Ekron and Ashdod are villages with a few cactus hedges; Ascalon lies in ruins by the sea; Gath is so little remembered that its name has disappeared, and its site become uncertain.

332. EKRON, the northernmost of the five chief Philistine cities, is memorable only as being the last place to which the "Ark of God" was taken before its return to Israel (1 Samuel v. 10).

333. GATH, "the city of giants," died out with the giants. It probably lay inland in the north of Philistia. When the Ark was taken from Ashdod, it was brought to Gath (1 Samuel v. 8).

334. Ashdod was the centre of the worship of the Philistine idol Dagon, and thither the Philistines bore in triumph the

"Ark of God" which they captured from the Israelites at the battle of Ebenezer (1 Samuel v. 1).

335. The Hebrew Ark proved to be a disastrous possession to the Philistines. The morning after it was placed in the temple of Dagon, the image of the idol was found prone on the ground (1 Samuel v. 4). Hurried off to Gath it brought trouble there; then to EKRON, it brought trouble there; and after being carted about from village to village during seven months, it was brought back into the Hebrew territory and left "in its own place" (1 Samuel vi.).

336. All that remains of ASCALON is a landing-place between reefs at which ships occasionally touch. There may be seen also, at low water, two shallows of crescent shape, supposed to have been ancient moles, and at the bottom of the rocky basin explorers think they can trace the lines of a little dock.

337. The only Philistine city now of any size or importance is GAZA. It lies on and around a hill which rises about 100 feet above the plain, at a distance of three miles from the sea.

338. It was while on his way from Damascus to Gaza, sent thither by the Divine Spirit, that the Evangelist Philip fell in with and joined himself to the Ethiopian eunuch, who was reading the book of the prophet Isaiah as he travelled in his chariot. After preaching Christ to the eunuch, and on hearing his confession of faith in Christ as the Son of God, Philip baptized him in a pool or brook that was near (Acts viii. 26-40).

339. It is thought by Dr. Thomson and other authorities that the fine fountain, AIN-EL-HANIYEH, near Ashdod, may mark the spot at which the baptism of the Ethiopian eunuch by Philip the Evangelist took place.

340. The climate of GAZA is almost tropical, but there are no less than 15 deep wells in and near the city which provide water for the population and for their gardens and groves.

341. There are few palm-trees in Gaza now, but there is an extensive olive-grove lying to the north and north-east. Hence arises a considerable manufacture of soap which is exported in large quantities. It has also an active trade in corn.

342. Gaza has bazaars for the sale of cloth, pottery, and weapons,—articles freely purchased by the Bedouins. As from Damascus, so from Gaza, great trade-routes led to and from Egypt, Petra, Palmyra, and Arabia.

343. Along the road which runs from Gaza to Egypt Joseph may have led Mary and the child JESUS in the flight into Egypt. Strange to say, telegraph wires now run along that old-world highway.

344. Gaza was the scene of more than one of Samson's wonderful feats. He once carried away its huge gates (Judges xvi. 3), and at Gaza he died, crushed with hundreds of his tormentors by the fall of the "House" or temple of Dagon, the pillars of which he tore down (Judges xvi. 21-31).

345. A traditional site of the House of Dagon which Samson pulled down is shown at Gaza. Dr. Geikie says it was a building bordered by colonnades, having a flat roof which projected beyond it, supported by pillars, thus forming a verandah. On this verandah the great ones of Gaza were crowded to see the Hebrew giant "make sport" for them in the open space below—sport which meant death to them and to their victim.

346. Four miles south-east of EKRON, you enter the "SAMSON COUNTRY." Mounting a hill which rises slowly from the Wady-es-Surar, Sorek, the ancient Zorah is reached, about 12 miles from Ekron. This was the birth-place of the famous Hebrew giant (Judges xiii. 24-25).

347. There is still a well at ZORAH, and many a time the boy Samson may have gone with his mother to this well as she went to fetch water for the household, carrying a water pot upon her head or shoulder.

348. After the destruction of the temple of Dagon at Gaza, Samson's kinsfolk and friends brought his body to his native village to find its last resting-place (Judges xvi. 31) in the land where he had spent his youth, and where first "the Lord blessed him, and the Spirit of the Lord began to move him" (Judges xiii. 25).

349. The Philistine and Samson country used to be one unbroken field of corn. It was, and is now, infested with jackals—called in the Old Testament foxes. It would be

easy for Samson to get any number of jackals, to set fire to such a plain of corn at harvest time (Judges xv. 4-5). Even at this day, rigorous precautions are taken by farmers against conflagrations.

350. The incident of the swarm of bees in the dried-up skeleton of the lion is true to experience in the Samson country. A dead camel is often found dried up by the summer heat, the mummy remaining unaltered and without any offensive smell (Judges xiv. 5-9).

351. In sight of Zorah, across the Valley of Sorek, is BETHSHEMESH (1 Samuel vi. 12), the house or city of the Sun, whither the "Ark of God" was brought after it had been dragged from place to place in the Philistine country.

352. The head of the Valley of Sorek has usually been considered to be the scene of the battle in which the Philistines captured the Ark. In carrying it back to Bethshemesh the Philistines may have desired to make atonement for their reckless conduct in dragging it about their own country. The stone on which they rested the Ark may have been the EBEN-EZER, or "stone of help" (1 Samuel vi. 14-15), which has so often been on the lips of Christians, and given a name to thousands of places of Christian worship.

353. As you travel the Philistine country you meet asses laden with all kinds of produce, and women and girls with milk, which they carry in jars on their shoulders. Married women sometimes carry their little children in the same way, and sometimes on their hips; just as Isaiah says: "Thy daughters shall be nursed at thy side" (Isaiah lx. 4).

354. Isaiah says that in the days of the Messiah "the lion shall eat teben like an ox" (Isaiah xi. 7). Teben is finely broken-up straw, brought in bags on camels from Egypt through the Philistine country to Joppa and other towns.

355. The Philistine country was once the country of the sycamore fig-tree, much more so than even the neighbourhood of Jericho. The sycamore fig-tree grows to a height of from 40 to 50 feet, having a thick gnarled stem and numerous strong limbs which, at a short distance from the ground,

strike out horizontally. It is thus easy to understand why Zacchæus of Jericho climbed into one of these trees to secure a suitable elevation from which he might see Jesus over the heads of the crowd in the road (Luke xix. 4).

356. Wherever the sycamore fig-tree grows in Palestine, children may be seen amusing themselves by getting up into its strong spreading branches, which provide a cool shade for those who choose to sit or recline beneath them.

THE DAVID COUNTRY.

357. The Valley of Sorek leads from the district, made famous by the exploits of Samson, into the district made famous by the exploits of David.

358. In the low hills south-east of Ashdod is the VALLEY OF ELAH, where David slew Goliath in the presence of the Hebrew and Philistine armies (1 Samuel xvii. 2). This Valley is now called the WADY-ES-SUNT—"the Valley of the Acacia."

359. The sling—the simple weapon by which David killed Goliath—is still in use among the shepherds in Palestine, not only to drive off wild animals, but to guide their flocks. "A stone cast on this side or that, before or behind, drives the sheep or goats as the shepherd wishes."

360. Two miles south of the Valley of Elah is the CAVE OF ADULLAM, where David once dwelt and attracted to his service a motley force consisting of "every one that was in distress, and every one that was in debt, and every one that was discontented" (1 Samuel xxii. 1-2).

361. The celebrated Cave of Adullam, writes Major Conder, "is a small one blackened with the smoke of many fires, and scooped on the side of a low hill on which are remains of a former town or village." When Conder visited the cave he found a poor family actually living in it.

362. The method of ploughing in the David Country reminds us of Elisha, "who was ploughing with twelve yoke of oxen before him, and he with the twelfth," which means that there were twelve ploughs at work, the twelfth being guided by the prophet himself (1 Kings xix. 19).

363. The country of David's early exploits is the country of the olive, a tree cultivated in Palestine long before the Hebrew settlement; it is as much a characteristic of Judæa as is the date-palm of Egypt.

364. The olive-harvest is in October, when the dark-green berries are gathered by women and boys who climb into the trees and beat the branches with poles.

365. To the poor olive-gleaners are left the berries that do not fall at the first gathering; this is as Moses commanded: "When thou beatest thine olive-trees thou shalt not go over the boughs again: it shall be for the stranger, the fatherless and the widow" (Deut. xxiv. 20).

366. The wealth of the olive is its oil. In ancient times the gathered berries were trodden by the feet in a vat, but the finest oil was that which flowed from the rich ripe berries when they were merely beaten, not from those which had to be trodden. Only the finest oil was used in religious services.

367. The numerous shoots springing up from the roots of the olive-tree furnished a pleasant poetical figure to the Psalmist: "Thy children," he wrote, "shall be like olive-plants round thy table," which means they will cluster round the family table as the olive-shoots cluster round the root from which they spring (Psalm cxxviii. 3).

368. Harvest operations in Judæa are little altered. The sickle is still used for reaping as it was in Old Testament times. When the reaper, and the binder who follows him, have done their work, asses or camels bear away the sheaves to the threshing-floor.

369. The threshing-floor is always selected on an exposed spot, in order to catch the wind for winnowing. As in the case of the "floor" of Araunah, the Jebusite, which was on Mount Moriah, flat spaces on hill-tops are preferred (2 Samuel xxiv.).

370. When the grain is finally winnowed, sifted, and thrown up into a heap, the farmer often takes up his quarters on the threshing-floor for the night, just as Boaz (Ruth iii. 7) did, ages ago, to keep watch over it.

371. The SOUTH COUNTRY is full of underground cisterns, formerly used for storing grain, their mouths being hidden

with a layer of soil to prevent discovery by a robber or an enemy. It was to such grain stores the men of Shiloh referred when pleading for their lives with Ishmael: "Slay us not, for we have treasures in the field, of wheat, of barley, of oil, and of honey" (Jeremiah xli. 8).

THE COUNTRY OF THE PATRIARCHS.

372. Travelling southward and eastward we come more and more among the sheep-farms, where the shepherds, like Jacob, and like the shepherds of Bethlehem in our Lord's time, abide in the fields, "keeping watch over their flocks by night" (Luke ii. 8).

373. GERAR, which has been identified in the present UMM-EL-JERRAR is the centre of the district in which the patriarch Isaac lived during nearly the whole of his quiet uneventful life, as a rich farmer and sheep-owner.

374. The shepherd of Palestine awakes with the dawn of day. Then he "putteth forth" his sheep, counting them as he lets them pass slowly under his rod, through the doorway of the fold. To help in doing this necessary work he "calleth his own sheep by name" (for other shepherds may have sheep in the same fold), "and leadeth them out" (John x.).

375. In the mountainous districts, cleft as they are by narrow and often impassable ravines, a sheep may easily wander too near the edge and fall into the depth below. In such places the shepherd carefully leads his flock, often looking back; and if he sees a sheep creeping too close to the ravine, he retraces his steps, approaches it, puts his crook round one of its hind legs and gently pulls it towards him.

376. In lambing-time the greatest care is taken of his flock by the shepherd. The ewes are led slowly, and you may often see him carrying one lamb in his arm, and another in the bosom of his cotton garment, below which is his well-fastened girdle. So the prophet pictures the Messiah: "He shall feed His flock like a shepherd; He shall gather the lambs with His arm, and carry them in His bosom, and shall gently lead those that are with young" (Isaiah xl. 11).

377. Flocks of goats are numerous in Judæa, and indeed in all Palestine, as they were in former ages. They may be seen everywhere in the mountains, a he-goat probably leading the flock,—a fact which may have prompted Jeremiah, Zechariah, and Daniel to speak of kings as the "he-goats of the earth" (Jer. li. 40; Zech. x. 3; Dan. viii. 8).

378. The quarrelsomeness of the he-goats in Palestine is proverbial. It often compels the shepherd to separate them from the meek and patient sheep, and it may have suggested the separation of the goats from the sheep in Christ's picture of the Day of Judgment (Matt. xxv. 32).

379. The country from Gerar to BEERSHEBA is much the same as that between Gaza and Gerar; low hills with herds of cattle; plains with flocks of sheep; now and then a few black tents; and here and there poor shepherds and Arabs on horseback, sometimes partly and sometimes completely armed.

380. When Palestine was divided among the tribes, Beersheba was assigned to Judah; but it was afterwards made over to Simeon, and became the southern limit of the possessions of the Israelites. "From Dan to Beersheba" was the extent of the land from north to south.

381. Beersheba must once have been a place of considerable importance; for in Samuel's day a local court was held there for the South Country under Abiah, the son of the prophet (1 Samuel viii. 2).

382. Beersheba was the centre of that pastoral country for ever renowned as the home of the first three and greatest Hebrew patriarchs, Abraham, Isaac, and Jacob. There Abraham settled after long wandering through the length of Palestine. There Isaac passed his quiet life. There Jacob was born, and from that place he went down into Egypt at the request of Joseph, who had become Pharaoh's Prime Minister.

383. In Beersheba the Chief of the tribe still dwells in his tent amidst his people and retainers as Abraham did. His sons and daughters tend the herds and flocks. The native Bedouin builds a stone pillar "for a memorial" as Jacob did; and still the Arab hunter brings back venison to the tent as Esau did.

384. The chief objects of interest at Beersheba are its wells. Standing by them and looking northward you see the same low hills which the patriarchs saw and the very fields into which Isaac used to go forth to pray.

385. The wells at Beersheba are now three in number; each is a round shaft lined with masonry.

386. The principal supply of water at Beersheba is from the largest of the three ancient wells; it is 12 feet 3 inches in diameter, and 38 feet deep to the surface of the water. The smallest of the wells is dry.

387. There is no parapet or wall to protect the wells at Beersheba, but there are rough stone troughs round the two which contain water,—nine round the larger one, and five round the smaller.

388. Beersheba was so called from the agreement made respecting it between Abraham and its Philistine owners. The two parties confirmed the bargain by a mutual oath and the gift of seven sheep from Abraham to Abimelech (Genesis xxi. 27). In allusion to this transaction Beersheba means either "well of the oath" or "well of the seven."

389. It was at Beersheba that Elijah, fleeing to Horeb to escape the vengeance of Jezebel, left his attendant and went a day's journey further south, and as the Bible relates, "he lay and slept" (1 Kings xix. 3) under a bush of broom, a plant common in the district; for it was not as the Authorized Version of Scripture has it, under a juniper tree.

HEBRON AND ITS SURROUNDINGS.

390. From Beersheba northward to Hebron, the track is through a rough valley called the **Hebron Valley**. The whole route is a long hard ascent, but through a deeply-interesting district, containing mementoes of a long past civilization.

391. HEBRON is not only the oldest town in Palestine, but one of the oldest in the world. When Josephus wrote, it was at least 2,500 years old.

392. Hebron was originally known as KIRJATH-ARBA, from Arba, father of Anak, the giant. In Abraham's time it was called MAMRE, after Mamre the Amorite (Joshua xiv. 15).

393. It was at the gate of Hebron Abraham publicly purchased the field of Machpelah " in the presence of the children of Heth " (Genesis xxiii. 3).

394. From Hebron Joseph was sent by his father, Jacob, to search for his brethren who were with the flocks in Shechem; and to Hebron those brethren came back to Jacob, bringing Joseph's blood-stained "coat of many colours" (Genesis xxxvii.).

395. Hebron was taken by Joshua only after a fierce and bloody struggle (Joshua x. 36-37). Subsequently Joshua gave it to Caleb as a reward for faithfulness (Joshua xv. 13). Later, it was made one of the cities of refuge to which the man-slayer might flee.

396. At Hebron David resided for seven years and a half (2 Samuel ii. 11), when he reigned over Judah only. There Absalom was born, and Abner was treacherously murdered by Joab. It was at the grave of Abner, "a Prince and a great man in Israel," that David "lifted up his voice and wept" (2 Samuel iii. 32).

397. To Hebron Absalom came, under pretence of fulfilling a vow, but really to seize the sovereignty of the kingdom; for he sent spies "through all the tribes of Israel, saying,—As soon as ye hear the sound of the trumpet then ye shall say—Absalom reigneth in Hebron" (2 Samuel xv. 10).

398. The modern name of Hebron is EL-KALIL, the Arabian for "the friend," in remembrance of the patriarch Abraham, who was called "the friend of God." Hebron is situated in the Valley of Eschol—so famous for its vineyards.

399. The present inhabitants of Hebron are chiefly Mahometans; they number about 12,000, of whom less than 1,000 are Jews. There are few, if any resident Christians.

400. Hebron has now no walls, but there are one or two useless old gates still standing. Its streets are dark and dirty, but the houses are for the most part substantial stone buildings, with many cupolas or small domes which help to give the place an attractive appearance.

401. The chief occupations of the Hebron people are the manufacture of rings and bracelets, some articles of domestic use, and the trinkets commonly found in eastern bazaars.

402. Hebron is supplied with water from two pools of very ancient date. To one of these allusion is made in the sentence pronounced by David upon the sons of Rimmon, who brought to him the head of Ish-bosheth, son of Saul, thinking to gratify him. But David was outraged, and he commanded his young men to slay them as he had before slain the man who brought him the tidings of the death of Saul (2 Samuel iv.)

403. Hebron is intensely interesting, both to Jews and Christians, because of the CAVE OF MACHPELAH, the burial place of Abraham, Isaac, and Jacob; Sarah, Rebecca, and Leah.

404. The CAVE OF MACHPELAH is no longer a cave in the midst of a field, but a Mosque, a massive stone building which no Christian may enter, and guarded with zealous care by its Mahometan owners.

405. Describing the Mosque at Hebron which covers the cave of Machpelah, Major Conder says: "Six cenotaphs stand in the enclosure, two inside the Mosque, two in chapels beside the porch of the same, and two in buildings against the rampart-walls." These are not the real tombs of the patriarchs and their wives; they only mark the sites of their tombs beneath the floor.

406. Only about a dozen Christian visitors have been allowed to enter the Mosque at Hebron, of whom the Prince of Wales, his son, and the late Dean Stanley are the best-known to Englishmen. An admirable account of what they saw was published by the Dean.

407. Besides the Cave of Machpelah, there is about a mile from Hebron an old oak-tree, or rather a terebinth-tree, called the Oak of Mamre, and venerated by vast numbers of enthusiasts as the very oak under which Abram pitched his tent.

408. The Oak of Abram, at Mamre, near Hebron, stands before a Russian hospice, erected there for the benefit of Pilgrims. The enormous tree is 34 feet in circumference

near the ground. At the height of 20 feet it divides into several large limbs, some vigorous, some decayed and leafless, spreading out to a distance of between 80 and 90 yards round the trunk.

409. Dr. Geikie, describing the Oak of Mamre, writes: "It is easier to say it is the tree under which Abram pitched his tent than to prove it, for it is quite certain that this particular tree, though it has been worshipped for 300 years as Abram's Oak, is only of yesterday compared with the long ages since the patriarch's time."

410. The country around Hebron, for miles in every direction, was the favourite pasture-land of the patriarchs. There they reared cattle and sheep in immense numbers, and prospered so well that they became rich and powerful princes of the district.

411. Hebron was, and still is, famous for its wine. It is very cheap, a bottle of it costing about sixpence of our money.

NORTHWARD FROM HEBRON THROUGH THE WILDERNESS.

412. The road from Hebron to Jerusalem has every appearance of having always been the highway between the two cities. Rough, unkempt, toilsome in every part, it is "simply fearful in some places, running in the dry bed of a torrent strewn with stones of all sizes."

413. The journey from Hebron to Jerusalem reveals a country and scenes which vividly recall Old Testament descriptions. Every spot, every object, and every person may be said to be Biblical in appearance and character.

414. As in old times, the ass is the main help for a journey in Judæa, horses being few, and mules used only for luggage and other burdens.

415. The stalwart native of Judæa, riding on a small donkey, is a common sight. Now and then a woman and a child are seen on the family ass, while the husband walks at the side of his wife. Thus Joseph travelled with Mary and

the child Jesus from Bethlehem to Egypt, and back from Egypt to Nazareth.

416. About three miles north of Hebron a path leads to TEKOA, memorable as the home of the prophet Amos, one of the humblest, but one of the greatest of God's messengers to Israel. "I was no prophet," was the modest description of himself given by Amos to Amaziah, "neither was I a prophet's son, but I was a herdman, and a dresser of sycamore trees, and the Lord took me from following the flock, and the Lord said unto me, Go, prophesy unto my people Israel" (Amos vii. 14-15).

417. The country between Hebron and Tekoa is the Wilderness which has for its eastern boundary the Dead Sea. Its general name is JESHIMON, which begins at Idumæa in the south and ends at the wild district between Jerusalem and Jericho in the north.

418. The Wilderness due east of Hebron is called the WILDERNESS OF JERUEL. There Jehoshaphat went out to meet the invading Moabites and Ammonites and their allies, the most dangerous foes the Hebrews ever encountered. Finding them already slaughtered in a valley, the delighted Judæans gave it the name of the Valley of Berachah, "the Valley of Blessing" (2 Chron. xx. 26).

419. North-east of Hebron and of Tekoa the country is a "dreary desert." Tekoa is now a camping place for wandering Arabs. Just as in Ishmael's days, these "children of the desert" roam through the land as they please, feeding their flocks on the open hill-sides and the thin grass of the plains.

420. A shepherd's life in the wilderness of Judæa is a hard life, as hard as that of his sheep or his goats. He cannot leave them day or night, and often he has no shelter. When tired of watching he will gather branches of shrubs and try to make a dry spot on which to stand or recline, in the wilder weather a sheep-skin or an old rug being his only coverlet. Perhaps it fared thus with shepherds of Bethlehem 1,900 years ago, when they were "abiding in the field, keeping watch over their flocks by night" (Luke ii. 8).

421. Into the wilderness of Judæa the jackal and the wolf still come, when food is scarce in their usual lairs.

In ancient times the lion also scoured it, as Amos writes, coming up from the thickets of Jordan, in Hebrew "the yaar," the short scraggy shrub which covers much of the land, and where once there were boars and other wild beasts as well as lions (Amos iii. 4-8).

422. There is one wonderful oasis beyond the wilderness of Tekoa and close to the Dead Sea, namely ENGEDI, a famous place of resort, refuge, refreshment, and rest.

423. To reach Engedi you have to travel seven hours without finding a water-spring or seeing a bush. Then, suddenly, over the edge of a precipice, 400 feet below you, you "see a river of verdure burst from the rock, and scatter itself amidst reeds, bush, trees, and grass, down other 300 feet to a broad terrace of gardens by the beach of the blue sea." You reach Engedi "through gardens of cucumber and melon, small fields of wheat and a scattered orchard, a brake of reeds, and high bushes with a few great trees."

424. Engedi, like Gaza and Jericho, was famous for its palm-trees; hence its name, "Hazazon-Tamar"—Hazazon of the Palm; but the palm, like the vine, has disappeared from Engedi.

425. Palm-branches have been from the remotest ages the symbol of rejoicing, the people of Palestine, like other peoples, using them to express general gladness, as when our Lord made His triumphal entry into Jerusalem the crowd of men, women, and children, took branches of palm and went forth to meet and accompany Him (John xii. 12-13).

MAR SABA AND SOLOMON'S POOLS.

426. Through the vast howling wilderness, called the wilderness of Judæa, at its northern end, we come to **Mar Saba,** famous for its convent, a gigantic building which, whether viewed from without or within, is one of the weird places of the world.

427. The convent of Mar Saba was founded by one SABAS, a man of great sanctity and learning, to whom was ascribed the power of working miracles. St. Sabas is said to have been born in Cappadocia A.D. 439.

428. Entering the convent of Mar Saba, the traveller finds himself in one of the strangest places ever contrived for human habitation. It is built upon a series of precipices, having walls of natural rock and artificial battlements. Many of its rooms are holes or caves of the rock. No woman is permitted to enter the convent.

429. Before reaching BETHLEHEM by the road from Hebron the traveller comes to a village called URTAS—the probable site of the ancient ETHAM. Josephus states that this place was 50 stadia from Jerusalem, and thither Solomon was "in the habit of taking a morning drive."

430. Etham, or Urtas, is beautiful still. It is probably of this place Solomon wrote in his book called "Ecclesiasties": "I made me great works; I builded me houses; I planted me vineyards; I made me gardens and parks; and I planted trees in them of all kinds of fruit; I made me pools of water, to water therefrom the forest, where trees were reared" (Eccles. ii. 4-6).

431. The Pools of Solomon are three enormous reservoirs of marble masonry, called the Upper, Middle, and Lower Pools respectively. Of these the latter is the largest, being 582 feet in length, 207 feet in breadth at its widest end, 148 at its narrowest, and 50 feet in depth.

432. The masonry of Solomon's Pools is still in excellent preservation. It was carefully repaired by Pontius Pilate.

433. Originally water was supplied from Solomon's Pools to Jerusalem. At present the water is only taken as far as Bethlehem, although the course of the aqueduct can be traced all the way to the court of the Temple, a distance of fully 12 miles.

BETHLEHEM.

434. About six miles north of Urtas, half way to Jerusalem, is BETHLEHEM, the birth-place of JESUS CHRIST, THE SAVIOUR OF MANKIND (Luke ii. 4).

435. Bethlehem, called in the Old Testament BETHLEHEM-EPHRATAH, stands on an elongated hill in the midst of cultivated cornfields, pastures and terraces. The whole

district is one of great fertility, having a good supply of water within easy distance.

436. The position of Bethlehem is one of considerable strength, and though as the prophet Micah said, "too little to be placed among the families of Judah" (Micah v. 2), Bethlehem has the finest site in the whole province of Judæa.

437. Bethlehem is frequently mentioned in the Old Testament; first of all, when Rachel died in giving birth to the child whom she named Benoni, "son of my sorrow," but whom Jacob named Benjamin, "son of my right hand." "And Rachel died," we read in Genesis xxxv. 19, "and was buried in the way to Ephrath, which is Bethlehem."

438. About a mile from Bethlehem is a small modern building which marks the spot where Rachel died and was buried. Jews, Christians, and Moslems alike revere the place as the authentic spot.

439. In Bethlehem and its surrounding fields is the scenery of the story of Ruth, who became the wife of Boaz, the mother of the kings of Judah, and the ancestress of the World's REDEEMER.

440. Bethlehem was the birth-place of David and the scene of many events in his chequered life. Here Samuel anointed him to be king of Israel. In the adjacent hill-country David tended sheep and defended the flocks from bear and lion and other wild beasts. Here David composed his earliest Psalms. From Bethlehem he was summoned by Saul to soothe that king's troubled soul by his melodious harpings.

441. Bethlehem was the place in which various members of the house of David distinguished themselves both in war-like exploits and works of peace; it was well called, therefore, "the city of David."

442. Quite near to Bethlehem, at the only spot where "a gate" could have been built, are three or four well-shafts, to the largest of which the name of "David's Well" is given. It was of the water of this well, "the well of Bethlehem, which is by the gate," that David, who was then at the head of the band of Adullamites, longed for a draught, a gratifica-

tion obtained for him at the risk of the lives of three of the mighty men of his motley army (2 Samuel xxiii. 15-17).

443. It was to Bethlehem that Joseph, the carpenter of Nazareth, came, with Mary his betrothed wife, to be taxed or counted in their "own city," in the census ordered by Cæsar Augustus, when Quirinius was governor of Syria (Luke ii. 3).

444. The supreme event in history, the event which has given to Bethlehem its crowning and immortal interest was the birth of JESUS CHRIST. This event occurred during the visit of Joseph and Mary. The evangelist Luke thus records it: "And it came to pass while they were there, the days were fulfilled that she should be delivered. And she brought forth her first-born son, and she wrapped him in swaddling clothes and laid Him in a manger, because there was no room for them in the inn" (Luke ii. 6-7).

445. When JESUS was born there was probably an unusual throng of strangers in Bethlehem, gathered there, as were Joseph and Mary, to be enrolled in obedience to the decree of Augustus. The upper-rooms of the Khan, or inn, were all occupied, and Joseph and Mary were compelled to accept accommodation in the place assigned to cattle, in the walls of which stone-mangers were built. Hence the birth-place of JESUS was a cattle-stall, and His first cradle a manger (Luke ii. 7).

446. Over what is called the "grotto of the Nativity" at Bethlehem a church was erected by the Empress Helena. Remains of that building, probably the most venerable Christian church in the world, are visible in the present structure. It was at first called the Church of St. Mary, but is usually called the Church of the Nativity.

447. From the transept of the Church of the Nativity steps descend to the grotto, or crypt, in which, it is asserted, the birth of Jesus actually took place; but there is no evidence that He was born in a grotto.

448. The grotto, or crypt, of the Nativity is marked by a large silver star set in the marble pavement. Around it is an inscription in Latin which says: "HERE JESUS CHRIST WAS BORN OF THE VIRGIN MARY." Near by is the manger,

or rather the place where it once was; for, according to tradition, the real manger was transported to Rome.

449. Describing the so-called grotto of the Nativity Dr. Thomson thus writes: "Everything is cased in marble, covered with silver and gold, surrounded with burning lamps, and pervaded with the odour of incense. There is nothing to remind one of the inn and the manger mentioned by Luke, or of the house where, according to Matthew, the Magi presented their offerings and their adoration to Him "who was born King of the Jews."

450. A short distance south of the Church of the Nativity is the "MILK GROTTO," the traditional place in which Mary and the infant JESUS were secluded before the flight into Egypt.

451. A short distance from the "MILK GROTTO" is the so-called house of Joseph; and beyond this the village of Beit-Sahûr, where the shepherds mentioned by Luke in his narrative of the Nativity are supposed to have resided.

452. After a walk of about fifteen minutes from the supposed site of Joseph's house, the "SHEPHERD'S FIELD" is reached. A very ancient tradition makes this the spot where the shepherds were "keeping watch over their flocks by night," when "the angel of the Lord came upon them, and the glory of the Lord shone round about them," and they received the "tidings of great joy" which were for all people (Luke ii. 8-10). A wall now encloses the Shepherds' Field in which there are some fine old olive-trees.

453. It was to Bethlehem the Magi—"wise men of the east," probably of the Zend or Persian religion—were led by a mysterious star, to find Him for whom the whole east was then looking, "the Desire of all nations." Having found Him they worshipped Him, and laid down before Him their pious gifts—"gold, frankincense, and myrrh" (Matt. ii.).

454. In Bethlehem and its neighbourhood occurred the "Massacre of the Innocents," which has given a supreme infamy to the name of Herod the Great. Jealous of the Child that was "born King of the Jews," and "mocked of the wise men" who did not go back to him from Bethlehem to report what they had witnessed, Herod "sent forth

and slew all the male children that were in Bethlehem, and in all the borders thereof, from two years old and under, according to the time which he had carefully learned of the wise men" (Matt. ii. 16).

455. In Bethlehem Jerome, the celebrated monk and hermit, lived for more than thirty years, drawn to it because it was the birth-place of the SAVIOUR of mankind. "Here," says the late Dean Stanley, "Jerome fasted, prayed, dreamed, and studied; here, too, he died and was buried."

456. Bethlehem is 100 feet higher than Jerusalem, being 2550 feet above the sea-level; but the hills around Bethlehem are lower than those which "stand round about Jerusalem."

457. The name Bethlehem means "House of Bread," but the Arabs call it Beit-lahm, which means "House of Flesh."

458. The present population of Bethlehem is estimated at between 4,000 and 5,000. The inhabitants are almost entirely Christians, associated with either the Latin, Greek, or Armenian churches. These sects live on good terms with each other.

459. Although Bethlehem was a walled town in the time of Boaz, when the elders "sat in the gate," there are no walls now. The streets are narrow and the houses all flat-roofed.

460. The flat-roofed houses of Bethlehem in many cases join each other as, indeed, they do in other Palestine towns. This explains our Lord's counsel to His disciples, not to think when troubles came on the land of coming down to take anything out of the house, if they chanced to be on the roof, but to flee along the continuous roofs and so escape (Matt. xxiv. 17; Mark iii. 15; Luke xvii. 31).

461. Many Palestine houses, like some in Bethlehem, have a flight of stairs outside leading to their flat roofs. When the paralytic man was brought to Jesus, those who carried him took him up the outside stairs to the house-top, and probably they let him down through a hatchway to the feet of the Saviour; for hatchway openings are not uncommon (Luke v. 19).

462. Sometimes men address a crowd in the street from the flat roof of a house. Christ told His disciples to use the house-tops for a pulpit from which to proclaim the good news He had brought to the world (Matt. x. 27; Luke xii. 3).

463. "An ordinary Bethlehem house, which is commonly a shop also," writes Dr. Geikie, "has usually one room of arched stone, without furniture, except the inevitable divan or broad seat along the wall, and the women show no timidity at your entrance. Squatted on the floor, one, it may be, is busy sewing while she watches her baby in the cradle; another is preparing to bake; a third will bring you a water-pipe and a glass of water, while you look over the crucifixes, rosaries, olive-wood boxes, mother-of-pearl carved shells, and little jars and cups of asphalt or red stone."

464. The modern shepherd of Bethlehem still tends his flock of long-eared, broad-tailed sheep, or lively black goats that browse in the fields under the shade of ancient olives. He is bare-legged, bare-armed, with huge slippers, and a white or coloured kerchief round his close-fitting skull-cap. His shirt is blue, reaching to his calves, and over it is a rudely-made "abba" or outer coat bound with a leather belt; he has a club to use against hyenas and other wild beasts, and a staff for the comfort and guidance of his sheep.

465. The women of Bethlehem, like the rest of their sisters in Palestine, disdain tattooing. They limit themselves to marks on the palms of the hands, between the eyes, and on the chin, with a row of small points along the lower lip, something like the old English "patch." They are for the most part handsome and good-looking.

466. Dr. Thomson says he was agreeably surprised and delighted at Bethlehem as he walked to the town from the Shepherds' Field, to hear some of Moody and Sankey's hymns sung in a school for girls.

467. It was near Bethlehem, in the district of Solomon's Pools, Dr. Thomson learned how Palestine crowds strew their garments before influential persons. The occasion was one of sadness, alas, rather than of joy, for the crowd which met the English Consul and his companion as they entered Bethlehem consisted of very poor peasants, who complained

bitterly of the exactions of their Turkish rulers. They did honour to the Consul by spreading their garments in his way.

468. On the top of a hill over against Bethlehem, named MAR ELIAS, is the MONASTERY OF ELIAS, where, say the monks who reside in it, Elijah rested in his flight from Jezebel.

JERUSALEM.

469. The road from Bethlehem to **Jerusalem** runs almost due north past Rachel's Tomb and the Monastery of Elias. The fine prospect from the Monastery shows to the south the white houses of Bethlehem on their height, and to the north, beyond a broad plain, the walls and buildings of Jerusalem.

470. Like every other traveller from the south to Jerusalem, Abraham would get a first glimpse of Mount Moriah from the elevation now called Mar Elias. It was on the third day of his painful journey from Beersheba to offer up his only son Isaac as a sacrifice to God that, lifting up his eyes, he saw the appointed place afar off. "Then Abraham said to his young men, Abide ye here with the ass; and I and the lad will go yonder and worship, and come again to you" (Genesis xxii. 5).

471. From Mar Elias the road to Jerusalem descends slowly until it reaches a low ridge which separates the VALLEY OF BETHLEHEM from the VALLEY OF REPHAIM OR HINNOM. From this ridge the traveller looking northward sees a white line crowning the horizon; it is the southern wall of the Holy City of the Jews, in their eyes "the city of God"— JERUSALEM, the most renowned city in the world.

472. A first sight of Jerusalem is deeply affecting, but not equally impressive from every point of view. The least impressive is that from the south; the most impressive is that from the east,—the sight seen by our Lord as He came from Bethany over the south-eastern shoulder of the Mount of Olives, on the day of His "triumphal entry" into the city.

F

473. Viewed either from the north, the north-east, or the east, Jerusalem justifies every description of it found in the Bible, even the proud boast of the writer of the 48th Psalm: "Beautiful for situation, the joy of the whole earth is Mount Zion. On the sides of the north, the city of the great king," and the no less jubilant words of the writer of the 125th Psalm: "As the mountains are round about Jerusalem, so the Lord is round about His people, from this time forth and for evermore."

474. On the north-east of Jerusalem rises MOUNT SCOPUS; on the east the MOUNT OF OLIVES; on the south-east the "MOUNT OF OFFENCE," so called because upon it Solomon built a palace for his heathen wives (1 Kings xi. 7-8); on the south is the "HILL OF EVIL COUNSEL," where, probably in one of the High Priest's houses, the priests and rulers of the Jews took counsel together to put Jesus to death.

475. The deep narrow valleys which surround Jerusalem on every side, except the north-west, are the "gorge-like glen of HINNOM" on the south; the NACHAL, or watercourse VALLEY OF KEDRON, called also the *Valley of Jehoshaphat*, on the east and north-east; and the VALLEY OF GIHON, with its pools on the west.

476. The VALLEY OF GIHON is on the west side of Jerusalem, and begins to descend from the Jaffa Gate southward, its eastern boundary being the hill of Zion. It was in this valley Solomon was crowned and proclaimed king, as we read in the First Book of Kings (i. 33-34). David said, "Cause Solomon my son to ride upon mine own mule, and bring him down to Gihon: and let Zadok the priest and Nathan the prophet anoint him king over Israel: and blow the trumpet, and say, God save king Solomon."

477. Not far from the Jaffa Gate, and below the height of Zion, there is a remarkable Pool, formed by the erection of stone barriers across the valley by squaring the rocky sides and clearing out the soil. On the level ground, higher up the valley, is another ancient Pool of smaller dimensions. These are the Upper and Lower Pools of Gihon. These structures are as old as the time of Hezekiah, who is said to have "stopped the upper water course of Gihon," and to

have "brought it straight down to the west side of the city of David" (2 Chron. xxxii. 30).

478. In the time of its greatest glory, Jerusalem is thought to have extended over seven hills—Gareb, Goath, Acra, Bezetha, Moriah, Zion, and Ophel. In our Lord's time it extended over the four last-named only.

479. The earliest reference in Scripture to Jerusalem is in Genesis xiv. 18, where it is called Salem, and Melchizedek is mentioned as its king. In the Book of Joshua it is called JEBUS; and in the Book of Judges, the "city of the Jebusites," after the people who then possessed it (Judges xix. 10-11).

480. In the time of Melchizedek, and also when held by the Jebusites, Jerusalem was little more than a mountain-fortress; and to visitors from the larger cities of modern Europe it presents much the same appearance to-day.

481. Jerusalem was not in the possession of the Hebrews until the time of the monarchy, so that it did not become their capital city until a comparatively late date in their history. More ancient centres of the national life were Hebron, Bethel, and Shechem.

482. Jerusalem has been a fortified city from first to last. "History and poetry," writes Dean Stanley, "are always recurring to her walls, and gates, and towers, as if responding to the Psalmist's invitation, 'Walk about Zion, go round about her, tell the towers thereof, mark well her bulwarks'" (Psalm xlviii. 12-13).

483. The stronghold taken by David (2 Samuel v. 6-9) from the Jebusites stood on Mount Zion. Repeated attempts were made by the Philistines and others to wrest it from him, but in vain. He was always victorious, and finally defeated them in the "Valley of Giants" near GIBEAH, or GIBEON, to the north of Jerusalem.

484. To the hill or height of Gibeon (2 Samuel vi. 3) David brought the Tabernacle constructed by Bezaleel and Aholiab; and there it remained until he had made a "new tent" for it on Zion. The sacred object removed thither, Zion became the great sanctuary of the nation.

485. It was in Gibeon the Lord appeared to Solomon in a dream, and asked what gift he desired. Reflecting upon his grave responsibilities and his human weakness, Solomon humbly compared himself to a little child, and piously asked for "an understanding heart," that he might judge the people righteously; a speech which pleased the Lord, and was graciously answered (1 Kings iii. 9).

486. David appears to have concentrated his efforts, and employed all his resources in enlarging and strengthening Jerusalem, so as to make it at once "a city of habitation" and an impregnable fortress. The only works of ornament which can be ascribed to him were the "Royal Gardens" on the level space where the Valleys of Hinnom and Kedron meet south-east of the city.

487. Solomon continued and multiplied the enterprises of his father, for the enlargement, ornamentation, and defence of Jerusalem. His three great works were—the Temple, with its east wall and cloisters, his own palace, and the Wall of Jerusalem.

488. On the east of Zion, not so lofty, and separated from it by the ravine called the TYROPŒON, or CHEESE-MAKERS' VALLEY, rose Mount Moriah, which, since the time of Solomon, if not of David, has been regarded as the most sacred ground in Jerusalem.

489. On Mount Moriah Solomon built the Temple, which was his greatest work, and has ever since borne his name. To provide a suitable site for the building, it was requisite to level the summit, an enterprise involving enormous labour; equally enormous was the cost of the completed structure (2 Chron. iii. 1).

490. To the Temple Solomon removed the Ark, and all the rest of the sacred objects of the Tabernacle, to remain evermore in the innermost chamber of the building, which was accounted the most gorgeous, and, by the Hebrews, the most sacred Temple in the world.

491. Besides being a most splendid building, Solomon's Temple was also a fortress of massive foundations, with gateways on every side. Its walls, great and high, and its gates of precious metals and stones, furnished the chief images in

descriptions of the heavenly Jerusalem both in the Old and New Testaments.

492. Perhaps the most arduous enterprise of David and Solomon was the provision of an adequate and permanent supply of water, not only for the use of the inhabitants in every part of Jerusalem, but also for the daily requirements of the Temple. The underground reservoirs and channels discovered in recent explorations, and the gigantic "Pools" constructed by King Solomon at Urtas, are the admiration of modern engineers and builders.

493. The splendid works of Solomon imposed burdens upon the people which they did not long bear. Even before Solomon's death, Jeroboam, the son of Nebat, the ambitious "overseer" of Ephraim, fomented a rebellion under the plea of resistance to cruel taxes; a rebellion which, in the reign of Rehoboam, Solomon's son and successor, grew into the revolt of the Ten Tribes, and ended in the division of the kingdom.

494. With the revolt of the Ten Tribes the Samaritans became a separated people. Sanctuaries were established in their own territory, and eventually they built a national Temple on Mount Gerizim.

495. Always exposed to the inroads of the heathen nations on the other side Jordan, and cursed with a long succession of bad monarchs, the kingdom of Israel or Samaria was finally overthrown by the Assyrians; its capital was taken, and the remnant of the people carried away into Mesopotamia and Media. Thus were the words of the prophet fulfilled: "The Virgin of Israel is fallen; she shall rise no more" (Amos v. 2).

496. Four hundred years after Rehoboam, in the reign of Jehoiachin of Judah, Jerusalem suffered a ruinous seige at the hands of Nebuchadnezzar of Babylon. The fall of the city was followed by the transportation of the Jews to Babylon and their "great captivity" (2 Kings xxv.; 2 Chron. xxxvi.).

497. After being captives in Babylon for 50 years, the Jews were set free by Cyrus the Great, who thereby proved himself to be their "deliverer." They returned to Jerusalem

and, first under Ezra and then under Nehemiah, the work of resettlement and restoration was carried on.

498. Slowly, and amidst great hardships was Jerusalem rebuilt and repeopled, and a new Temple reared, after the Babylonish captivity. How the work was done, Nehemiah tells in the Old Testament book which bears his name.

499. Notwithstanding the work of restoring Jerusalem and reviving the ancient worship, accomplished by Nehemiah, the Jews knew not a single generation of peace during the following 500 years. Often torn to pieces by internal quarrels, they were the prey of Persian, Grecian, Syrian, and Egyptian enemies in turn.

500. Under the Syrian monarch, Antiochus Epiphanes, Jerusalem experienced a supreme insult. He consecrated the Temple to the worship of Jupiter, and sacrificed swine (which were an abomination to the Jews) upon its sacred altar.

501. In the time of the degradation of Jerusalem, under Antiochus, there lived in Modin, a little town of Judæa, one Mattathias, a man faithful to the law and ready to die in its defence. Refusing to worship the gods of Syria at the king's command, Mattathias had to flee with his wife and his sons to the "hill country." Those sons were the famous Jewish patriots, known as the Maccabees, so called after the brother named Judas, or Maccabæus—"the Hammer."

502. It was Judas Maccabæus, Judas "the Hammer," who defeated the Syrians at Beth-horon, a rocky height on the border of Samaria and Judæa, at or near which, 1,500 years before, Joshua won a great fight against the Canaanites, on the day when "the Sun stood still upon Gibeon and the Moon stayed in the Valley of Ajalon, until the people had avenged themselves on their enemies" (Joshua x. 12-13). Gibeon and the Valley of Ajalon are near Beth-horon.

503. Had it not been for the heroic efforts of the Maccabees to free the Jewish people from the tyranny of Syria, their religion would have been abandoned and their nationality lost.

504. Under their family name of the Asmoneans, Judas Maccabæus and his successors ruled in Jerusalem for a

period of 120 years, repairing the city and the Temple, and restoring the Hebrew worship and Levitical institutions.

505. After a chequered tenure of authority the Maccabean or Asmonean rule came to an end. The later members of it became involved in family feuds and personal quarrels; the last of them was dethroned and succeeded by the Idumæan Herod—best known as Herod the Great—in the year 40 B.C.

506. Jerusalem found another rebuilder, at once enterprising and munificent, in Herod the Great, who, as if striving to emulate Solomon, restored and ornamented it in a style of great splendour.

507. In our Lord's time Jerusalem was fortified by two walls—the first, or most ancient wall, enclosed the whole of Mount Zion and the lower part of the ridge of Mount Moriah, below the Temple, as far as Siloam. The second, or Hezekiah's wall, started from a point near the Tower of Hippicus, and encompassed the northern quarter of the city as far as Fort Antonia. A third, or outer wall, was afterwards built by Agrippa, to enclose a populous suburb called Bezetha, or "the New City," which had extended to the north of the second wall.

508. Within the old wall, at the north-west corner, stood the palace built by Herod the Great upon the old site of the palace of David; it was extensive and splendid, with cloisters, gardens, fountains, and a lofty enclosing wall.

509. Near his palace, and on the old wall, Herod built three towers of great size and magnificence—Hippicus, Phasaëlus, and Mariamne. Hippicus, which still forms a part of the fortifications, and greets the traveller as he enters the city by the Jaffa Gate, is the only building which has survived the overthrow of Jerusalem by Titus.

510. Herod enlarged and strengthened the Tower of Baris, which stood at the north-west angle of the Temple. This fortress, which he called Antonia, in honour of his friend and patron Mark Antony, communicated with the Temple by a flight of steps, so that the Roman soldiers might have easy access to the sacred building, and suppress any disturbance which might arise at the religious feasts.

511. The fortress of Antonia was the Prætorium of Pilate mentioned by the evangelist John (xviii. 28). Here our Lord and Saviour was brought before the Roman procurator; here, at the command of Pilate, He was scourged with thongs; here He was mocked by the soldiers, who put a reed in His hand for a sceptre, a scarlet robe over His shoulders, and a crown of thorns on His head.

512. Standing on the steps connecting the fortress of Antonia with the Temple court, and protected by the Roman soldiers from the Jews who sought to do him violence, the Apostle Paul delivered the famous address recorded in the twenty-second chapter of Acts. On his declaring that God had sent him to the Gentiles, the mob became the more enraged, whereupon the captain ordered him to be brought into the castle and examined by scourging; an infliction which he prevented by the startling declaration that he was a Roman born, and could not be lawfully punished untried and uncondemned.

513. Herod rebuilt the Temple on the old site. It was a vast structure of outer and inner courts and cloisters, lying "four square," with a gate on each side, each gate an elaborate and costly work of art, one, the "Beautiful Gate" being a marvel of design and precious materials.

514. Within the two outer courts of the Temple, standing upon a richly tesselated floor of its own, and approached by steps of marble as white as that of its walls, through gates and porches with pillars and domes of wonderful grace and beauty, rose the "Golden Temple," the inner Shrine, in which were the priceless objects used in worship,—Divine heirlooms of the Hebrew race,—and that most mysterious and awful sanctuary the "Holy of Holies," which the High Priest only might enter.

515. While buildings of regal magnificence and luxury arose elsewhere in Palestine, as at Shechem and Samaria, Jerusalem only was entitled to be called "a city of palaces." When enlarged and adorned by Solomon, it was incomparably superior to any other Hebrew city; and after its embellishment by Herod the Great, it is probable that no city in the east except Antioch, and no city of the west except Rome, equalled Jerusalem in external splendour.

516. To the Temple at Jerusalem the infant Jesus was brought forty days after His birth by Mary and Joseph to be presented before the Lord in the same manner as the other first-born sons of Jewish mothers; and there He was recognised by the saintly Simeon and the prophetess Anna as none other than the promised Messiah (Luke ii.).

517. To the Temple at Jerusalem Jesus, as a boy of twelve, came with His parents to keep the Passover. Day after day, during the feast, He would witness the gorgeous ritual and the offering of sacrifices, and take part in the singing and responses of the Temple services; above all, He would delight to listen to the aged teachers, who sat among the pillars of the outer porches, as they taught and answered questions. Joseph and Mary having left Jerusalem, and discovering that Jesus was not with them returned to the city, and found Him in the Temple with the Rabbis, astonishing all who heard Him by His questions and answers (Luke ii.).

518. Our Lord went up to Jerusalem at the beginning of His public ministry, when He exercised the highest authority of a prophet and reformer by cleansing the Temple. Under the sanction of the priests, who profited by it, oxen and sheep and doves were sold within the sacred precincts; there, too, money-changers changed foreign coins into half-shekel pieces, the only money the priests would take in payment of the tax for Divine worship. Jesus drove the traders from the Temple, saying: "Make not My Father's house a house of merchandise" (John ii. 13-16).

519. About the middle of the Feast of Tabernacles, in the last year of His ministry, Jesus again appeared, teaching in the Temple. As He was teaching, the Pharisees and chief priests sent officers to take Him; but they, feeling the spell of His presence and heart-searching words, dared not execute their warrant; on returning to the chief priests and Pharisees, and being asked why they had not brought Him, they replied "Never man spake like this man" (John vii. 46).

520. The day after the ineffectual attempt to arrest Him, and in the Temple, the woman taken in adultery was brought to Jesus, her accusers seeking to entangle Him by a subtle problem respecting the legal penalty for her sin. Repelling

them, He stooped down and wrote with His finger on the ground, this being the only occasion on which He is reported to have written anything (John viii. 6).

521. The incident of the woman taken in her wickedness was followed by the controversy recorded in the eighth chapter of John's Gospel, when Jesus declared that He was greater than Abraham. "They took up stones therefore to cast at Him; but Jesus hid Himself and went out of the Temple" (John viii. 59).

522. During His last week in Jerusalem, called the "week of conflict," our Lord cleansed the Temple a second time; spoke the parables of the "Two Sons and the Vineyard," the "Wicked Husbandmen," and the "Wedding Garment;" answered the question put to Him by the Pharisees and the Herodians respecting the payment of tribute to Cæsar, and the question of the Sadducees as to marriage in the kingdom of heaven.

523. In the last day of the "great week of conflict" in Jerusalem, our Lord answered the Scribe who asked Him which was the greatest commandment of the law; declared the woes against the Scribes and Pharisees, and spake of the widow who put two mites into the treasury the immortal words: "This poor widow cast in more than they all; for all these did of their superfluity cast in unto the gifts; but she of her want did cast in all the living that she had" (Mark xii. 43-44).

524. It was the magnificent city rebuilt and adorned by Herod the Great which 40 years after our Lord had "gone away" suffered the most terrible siege that ever befel it, that of the Romans under Vespasian and his son Titus.

525. All through the siege of Jerusalem by the armies of Titus, besiegers and besieged alike fought with unsurpassed courage and persistence, the Jews resisting with all the tenacity of their race even when further efforts of defence were worse than useless; they yielded only to exhaustion and starvation, uncowed to the last by their superior numbers and weapons of their foes.

526. The destruction of Jerusalem by the Romans, the woe and ruin that would accompany and follow it, "the great tribulation such as had not been from the beginning of

the world" till then, were predicted by our Lord in the solemn words He spake to the disciples, when He sat with them on the brow of Olivet, contemplating the city two days before the Last Supper (Matt. xxiv. 21).

527. After the siege of Titus, Jerusalem slowly rose out of her ashes, and in sixty years she once more lifted her head in prosperity. Then her proud spirit of independence again asserted itself, a rebellion broke out, headed by one Bar-Cochba, and brought upon it another siege and overthrow by the legions of the Emperor Hadrian who, resolved, to utterly crush out every disposition to revolt, rebuilt the city after the western fashion, gave it the name of ŒLIA CAPITOLINA, and turned its Temple into a heathen shrine.

528. Although started on a new career, with a Gentile name and a pagan worship, the fortunes of Jerusalem did not brighten. When Constantine embraced Christianity, in the fourth century, he rebuilt it and opened it to Christians; in the seventh century the Saracen Caliph, Omar, captured it.

529. During the Crusades, Jerusalem was held alternately by Franks and Saracens, until Saladin finally drove the European forces out of Palestine. Later it was taken by Mehemet Ali, Pasha of Egypt; since when, it has been under the government of the Sultan of Turkey.

JERUSALEM AS IT IS.

530. A profound interest has been recently aroused in everything relating to God's ancient people—the Jews, their country, and their capital. So well-devised, so earnest, and so successful have been the labours of the "Palestine Exploration Fund," and of other societies and individual investigators—British, American, German, and French—that to-day we are better informed about few historical races than about the descendants of Abraham, and few countries than the land promised to Abraham and to his seed after him.

531. The terrible experiences of Jerusalem have been due mainly to the cruel hands of her besiegers; they have been due to earthquakes also, to two especially, one of which occurred in the reign of Uzziah and is forcibly described by

Josephus; the other occurred during the crucifixion of our Lord, and is briefly but most impressibly described in the 27th chapter of Matthew.

532. If Palestine is to-day a land of ruins, Jerusalem is as truly a city of ruins. The Jerusalem of Solomon lies buried under the debris of many sieges and captures; the "very soil on which the city stands is found to be composed of ruins of houses, aqueducts, and pillars, reaching to a depth of thirty or forty feet below the foundations of the present houses."

533. The present city of Jerusalem, although it contains some magnificent buildings is for the most part a scene of dirt and wretchedness; its houses are low and the streets narrow and muddy; swarms of dogs roam the streets at their pleasure, make a horrible noise and show their teeth at anyone who ventures to disturb their independence.

534. "The general appearance of Jerusalem is entirely changed on the occasion of the great annual festivals. Even now in her decay the city presents a strikingly picturesque appearance at Easter, when Christian pilgrims from the far west mingle with the many-coloured Arabs, Turks, Greeks, Latins, Spanish and Polish Jews, and crowd to suffocation the church of the Holy Sepulchre."

535. The present walls of Jerusalem, averaging 35 feet in height and surrounded by thirty-four towers, were built in the sixteenth century. The principal gates opened in the wall are: the Damascus-gate on the north, St. Stephen's-gate and the Golden-gate (now closed) on the east, the Dung-gate on the south, the Gate of David or Zion-gate at the south-west corner, the Jaffa-gate on the west, and the New-gate (only recently opened, 1889) between the Jaffa-gate and the Damascus-gate.

536. The city of Jerusalem is now divided into four principal quarters: the Christian quarter, where are the church of the Holy Sepulchre and the English church; the Armenian quarter, with its fine convent in the south-west; the Mussulman quarter, with its wretched bazaars in the north-east; and on the south-east the Jews' quarter, poor and pestilential.

537. Situated in the Christian quarter and in the heart of the present city of Jerusalem is the old and famous sanctuary, the church of the Holy Sepulchre, built originally by the Crusaders upon the traditional site of our Lord's tomb. Here millions have worshipped in simple faith, believing that the building covers the spot where our Lord was crucified, where He was buried, and where He revealed Himself after His resurrection.

538. On Mount Moriah, where once was the Temple, is now the Mosque of Omar, or the Dome of the Rock, standing within an enclosure called the Haram-es-Sherif, or the "Noble Sanctuary." Within the Mosque the rock itself, from which the monument takes its name, is the object of supreme interest; for this is the spot where Melchizedek worshipped; where Abraham brought Isaac as a sacrifice to God; where the Ark of the Covenant first stood after its removal from Zion, and where David pleaded for his plague-stricken people.

539. Though the Temple proper was utterly overthrown by the Romans, as our Lord foretold, still there remains a portion of the outer west wall of the Temple court, consisting of massive blocks of stone which are generally admitted to be relics of the ancient Temple built by Solomon. To this place, called the WAILING PLACE, the Jews come every Friday afternoon, and with sobs and tears read or chant the Psalms, or other portions of Scripture which predict how Zion shall be a wilderness and Jerusalem a desolation.

540. Near the Damascus-gate, on the north side of the city of Jerusalem, an entrance has been discovered leading by a low aperture to vast and spacious underground quarries; the rocky pillars left to prop up the roof resemble the massive columns of a Norman cathedral. From these quarries was obtained the stone used in building Solomon's Temple. Here the stones were hewn and prepared, each ready to be fitted into its place; for "there was neither hammer nor axe, nor any tool of iron heard in the house while it was building" (1 Kings vi. 7).

541. Near the Sheep-gate, now St. Stephen's-gate, on the east of the city of Jerusalem, is the probable site of the ancient Pool of Bethesda. It is now dry; but in our Lord's

time this pool, which had five porches to enter by and a roof over it, was used for bathing. At times the water moved; and, every day, poor, sick, lame, and blind people lay round the pool, believing that an angel moved the water and that whoever went in first would be healed.

542. It was at the Pool of Bethesda that our Lord found the poor man who had not walked for thirty-eight years, and had been carried every day for years to the pool, but always failing to get in first when the water moved. Our Lord healed him, saying, "Rise, take up thy mat, and walk" (John v. 2-9).

543. At the southern extremity of the Tyropæon Valley lies the famous POOL OF SILOAM; it is 52 feet long and 18 feet wide. Some broken columns and other fragments show that an edifice—probably a church—was once built over the Pool. Eight ancient stone steps, worn and polished by the footfall of ages, lead to the waters, which are used by the people for drinking, for washing their linen, and for bathing.

544. The waters of the Pool of Siloam, which was within the walls of the ancient city of Jerusalem, come from the Virgin's Fountain by means of a tunnel, 1750 feet in length, cut, probably in the time of Hezekiah, through the rocky hill of Ophel—a work of great labour. Another tunnel has been discovered of smaller dimensions but of more ancient date, built for the same purpose as the more recent one probably in the days of Solomon. To this smaller watercourse Isaiah refers in the words "the waters of Shiloah which go softly" (Isaiah viii. 6).

545. The waters which supply the Pool of Siloam, as well as the Virgin's Fountain, and the fountains which flowed in the Temple area, are supposed to have their source in a living spring beneath the Temple Mount. Of this never-failing supply the Psalmist sang, "There is a river, the streams whereof shall make glad the city of God, the holy place of the tabernacles of the Most High" (Psalm xlvi. 4).

546. It was to the Pool of Siloam that our Lord sent the blind man to wash his eyes: "He anointed the eyes of the blind man with clay and said, Go wash in the Pool of Siloam; he went his way and washed and came seeing" (John ix. 7).

547. During the Feast of the Tabernacles, in the later days of the Jewish nation, the priests, in commemoration of the miraculous stream which flowed from the rock under the rod of Moses, wound daily in long procession down the slope from the Temple to the Pool of Siloam to draw water in golden urns. They bore it back, the crowd surging around, and then, amidst the blast of trumpets and the tumult of rejoicing, poured it on the altar, whilst thousands of voices chanted Isaiah's words, "With joy shall ye draw water out of the wells of salvation" (Isaiah xii. 3).

548. On the last day of the Feast of Tabernacles, when the priests had concluded the joyous ceremony of fetching water from the Pool of Siloam and pouring it on the altar, Jesus, proclaiming Himself the giver of the water of life, stood before the multitude and cried; "If any man thirst let him come unto me and drink" (John vii. 37).

549. The modern VILLAGE OF SILOAM,—an Arab village with the name SILWAN, lies on the west side of the Valley of Jehoshaphat, and is perched on a very steep and slippery place cut in the face of the hill; it is a miserable place, the houses for the most part being built at the mouths of ancient tombs. Near here must have been the Tower of Siloam, of which we read that it "fell and slew eighteen persons" (Luke xiii. 4).

550. South of Siloam is an open space, where in ancient times David and Solomon had their royal gardens. To-day, the hollow, and the lower slopes at the sides are still covered with gardens, and even when the heat of summer has burned up the surrounding landscape these gardens and terraces watered by countless rills from the Pool are still richly green. Perhaps these gardens suggested to Jeremiah, who lived most of his life in Jerusalem, the words "Blessed is the man that trusteth in the Lord, and whose hope the Lord is. For he shall be as a tree planted by the waters, and that spreadeth out her roots by the river, and shall not see when heat cometh, but her leaf shall be green; and shall not be careful in the year of drought, neither shall cease from yielding fruit" (Jeremiah xvii. 7-8).

551. About a third of a mile from the Pool of Siloam, and situated on the west side of the Valley of Jehoshaphat,

is the Fountain of the Virgin; it lies at the bottom of two flights of stone steps—thirty in all—and has the glory of being the only spring rising in the Temple Mount. The fountain takes its name from a legend that here the Virgin Mary washed the swaddling clothes of the infant Saviour.

552. The waters of the Fountain of the Virgin have the curious feature of rising and falling at intervals. This peculiarity possibly marks it as the Dragon's Pool mentioned by Nehemiah (ii. 13); popular superstition supposing that the rise and fall of the waters were due to a gigantic water-monster in the hill, which drank up the stream and vomited it forth, in turn.

553. Situate on the south and south-west of the city of Jerusalem lies the Valley of Hinnom—"the valley of the groans of children": a deep and narrow ravine, with steep, rocky sides. This valley, filled in their season with fruit-trees, grain, and flowers, once witnessed the most cruel scenes, when, under Ahaz, Manasseh, and Amon, the Israelites offered their children upon the open hand of the hideous figure of Moloch, around which a heated furnace sent its flames. The name, Ge-Hinnom—"the Valley of Hinnom," slightly changed into "Gehenna," became the common name for the place of eternal torment.

554. At the eastern end of the Valley of Hinnom, and on the steep southern face of the valley, is ACELDAMA. When Judas took back the thirty pieces of silver, and cast them down in the Temple, and went and hanged himself, the chief priests, deciding that the money, being the price of blood, must not be put back into the treasury, bought with it "the Potter's Field to bury strangers in"; hence the place was called Aceldama, or "the Field of Blood" (Matt. xxvii. 6-8).

555. On the eastern side of the Valley of Jehoshaphat is the JEWS' CEMETERY. The slopes stretching from the foot of Olivet to the Kedron are all covered with tombs, amongst them being the well-known tombs of Zechariah, St. James, and Absalom; of these, the first two are chambers cut in the rock. The splendid tomb of Absalom, a square building, with columns against the walls, is now blocked up with stones, in Arab fashion, as a sign of disgust at the memory of David's ungrateful son.

556. The most probable site of GOLGOTHA, the scene of our Lord's crucifixion, lies just outside the north wall of the city of Jerusalem. The Hebrew name, GOLGOTHA, means "the skull," the Latin form of the word being "CALVARY." Not far from the Damascus Gate is a knoll of rock of rounded form, with two holes in the face of the rocky bank, much like the sockets of eyes. The resemblance of the hillock to a skull is such that we may almost certainly say it is of this place that Luke writes, "When they came unto the place which is called the Skull, there they crucified him" (Luke xxiii. 33).

557. The late General Gordon, Major Conder, and other eminent authorities, have, after careful investigation, accepted the skull-shaped knoll on the northern side of Jerusalem, near the Damascus Gate, as the place of the Crucifixion. A credible tradition makes it the ancient place of execution according to the law. The Moslems call it "El-Heidemiyeh," the Christians "Jeremiah's Grotto." It is now widely known as the "Gordon Site."

558. The "Gordon Site" of the Crucifixion was singularly appropriate for a public spectacle. It was "without the city wall," but clearly visible from it, with a natural amphitheatre of surrounding slopes. Singular to say, an ancient tomb has been discovered a little west of the site, the character of which leads the same authorities to think it may have been the garden tomb of Joseph of Arimathæa, in which our Lord was laid.

559. Of the identified roads and sites of the neighbourhood of Jerusalem, few can have deeper interest for Christians than the road to, and the site of, EMMAUS, whither two of His disciples, probably Cleopas and Luke, were journeying on the day of the Resurrection, when Christ joined them, conversed with them, and, after partaking of a meal with them, disappeared as suddenly as He had arrived (Luke xxiv.)

560. "Emmaus," says Josephus, "means a warm bath, useful for healing"; the name is probably a corruption of the Hebrew word "Hammath," implying the presence of a hot spring. The village of Emmaus was nearly eight miles from Jerusalem, but in what direction the New Testament does not indicate.

561. ARIMATHÆA, the town or village of that Joseph who provided a tomb for our crucified Saviour, has not been definitely identified. Dr. Robinson fixed its site at a little hamlet called Rantieh, in the district of Ramleh, in Judæa; but with better reason it is fixed at Ramah, "the height" in Samaria, famous as the birth-place, the home, and the burial-place of the prophet Samuel.

THE MOUNT OF OLIVES AND BETHANY.

562. The long mountain ridge, which rises close to Jerusalem on its eastern side, is known in both the Old and New Testaments as the **Mount of Olives**, or the Mount of the Olive Garden. The olives, and oliveyards, from which it derived its name, have almost disappeared; now it is only on the deeper and more secluded slope, leading up to the northernmost summit, that these venerable trees spread into anything like a grove.

563. The Mount of Olives has four peaks, or summits, bearing different names: the first is called the "Galilee," from the supposition that there the angels stood, as our Lord went away, who said to the disciples, "Ye men of Galilee" (Acts i. 11); the second, the "Ascension," because it is the supposed site of that great event; the third, the "Prophets," from the curious catacombs called the "Prophets' Tombs" on its side; the fourth, the "Mount of Offence," because there Solomon established the worship of idols.

564. The southern outlier of the Mount of Olives is the "HILL OF EVIL COUNSEL." Upon it is the famous wind-driven tree called the "Tree of Judas," from a branch of which it is pretended the betrayer hanged himself in remorse for his crime.

565. It is said in the Jewish Mishna that the Shechinah, or the Presence of God, having finally departed from Jerusalem, "dwelt" three years and a half on the Mount of Olives, to see whether the Jewish people would or would not repent, calling, "Return to me, O my sons, and I will return to you"; "Seek ye the Lord while He may be found, call ye upon Him while He is near"; and then, when all was in vain, the Presence "returned to its own place."

566. While it is almost useless to seek for traces of Christ's presence in the streets and buildings of modern Jerusalem, seeing that the city has been captured and laid waste ten times since He went away, it is impossible not to find them on the sides and pathways of the Mount of Olives.

567. A small stone bridge, of one low arch, crosses the Kedron Valley, between the Temple Hill and Olivet. A venerable chapel stands near the eastern side of the bridge, approached by a deep descent and a flight of steps. As the bridge is the only one that affords a way from the east side of Jerusalem to the Mount of Olives, it is rarely without passengers.

568. Not far from the bridge between the Temple and Olivet is the traditional site of the GARDEN OF GETHSEMANE, to which our Lord led the eleven disciples on the night of the institution of the Last Supper, where He suffered His agony, and where He was betrayed.

569. Dr. Geikie describes the present Garden of Gethsemane as an irregular square, 160 feet long and 150 feet broad, divided into flower-beds and protected by hedges. The monks make bouquets of flowers, crowns of thorns, and rosaries of pieces of olive and small stones, which they sell to visitors. Of the existing olive trees, Dean Stanley says that as long as they live "their gnarled trunks and scanty foliage will always be regarded as the most affecting of the sacred memories in or about Jerusalem."

570. On the eastern side of the Mount of Olives, perched upon a plateau of rock, screened from the view of the top of Olivet by an intervening ridge, is a wild mountain-hamlet: this is the BETHANY of the Gospel narratives, sacred to Christians as the home of Christ's intimate friends—Mary, Martha, and Lazarus.

571. Bethany is now called El-Azariyeh or Lazariyeh, a name derived from the traditional site of the one house and grave which give it an undying interest. A tomb is shown which is said to be the tomb of Lazarus—a poor chamber very unlike a Jewish tomb, to reach which you have to descend no fewer than twenty-six steps; a so-called site of the house of Mary and Martha is also pointed out.

572. Bethany is the last collection of human dwellings before the desert-hills which reach to Jericho. Here our Lord often rested after His labours in Jerusalem, and His conflicts with the Priests, Pharisees, and Rulers. Hither, too, He came every evening during the last week of His earthly life.

573. Looking eastward from Bethany you see the Peræan hills; the foreground is the deep descent to the Jordan Valley; on the further side of that dark abyss Martha and Mary knew that Christ was abiding when they sent a messenger to tell Him of the dangerous illness of Lazarus; up that long ascent He came when, outside the village, the sisters met Him, and the Jews stood round weeping (John xi. 3).

574. Immortalized by that "mighty work"—the raising of Lazarus—Bethany retains no small renown as being the place of residence of Simon, the rich leper, whom Jesus probably healed, and who entertained Him at a feast, at which the restored Lazarus was present, and Martha served, and Mary anointed Jesus, as the evangelist John records: "Mary, therefore, took a pound of ointment of spikenard, very precious, and anointed the feet of Jesus, and wiped His feet with her hair: and the house was filled with the odour of the ointment" (John xii. 3).

575. Three pathways lead from Bethany to Jerusalem; one a long circuit over the northern shoulder of Olivet, down the valley which parts it from Mount Scopus; another, a steep footpath over the summit; the third, the continuation of the road by which mounted travellers and caravans approach Jerusalem from Jericho, over the southern shoulder, between the summit which contains the "Tombs of the Prophets" and the Mount of Offence.

576. The southern road from Bethany to Jerusalem is still a broad and well-defined track, winding over rock and loose stones, a steep declivity below on the left, the sloping shoulder of Olivet above on the right, fig-trees growing here and there out of the stony soil. In a valley of fig-trees on this route, ruins have been found which are supposed to mark the site of BETH-PHAGE—"the House of Figs"—"phage" meaning "green figs."

577. It was along the southern road from Bethany that Christ made His triumphal entry into Jerusalem. After resting for the night with His friends in Bethany, He set forth riding upon an ass, the symbol of old-time Jewish royalty, accompanied by the crowd that had gathered at Bethany on the previous night, and who, proud of the "Prophet of Nazareth," whom they now believed to be the Messiah, escorted Him, testifying to the "mighty work" He had wrought at the grave of Lazarus.

578. Intelligence having reached Jerusalem of the resurrection of Lazarus and of the approach of Christ to the Holy City, a great crowd left it to meet Him and return with Him. As the people passed through the palm-gardens, they cut down branches, as was their custom at the Feast of Tabernacles, and advanced singing verses of Psalms in honour of the great Comer.

579. Meeting the Bethany crowd mid-way on the southern road, the Jerusalem crowd joined it, and the combined multitude went forward to the city, strewing palm-branches and throwing their loose outer garments in the way, and making the air ring with the exultant cry, "Hosanna to the Son of David: Blessed is He that cometh in the name of the Lord: Hosanna in the highest" (Mark xi. 9-10).

580. Arrived within sight of the City—"even at the descent of the Mount of Olives"—some discordant cries were heard from the Pharisees amidst the acclamations of the multitude: "Rebuke Thy disciples" was one of the cynical appeals made to Him. "And He answered and said, I tell you that, if these should hold their peace, the stones would cry out" (Luke xix. 40).

581. Coming nearer to the City, probably to a point in the road which permitted a full view of the Temple walls, towers, and pinnacles, Christ wept over it and uttered the sad prediction of its capture and ruin, recorded by the evangelist Luke (Luke xix. 41-44).

582. It was on one of His journeys between Bethany and Jerusalem our Lord saw and blighted the fig-tree which had on it "nothing but leaves," the only act of destruction recorded of Him, thereby enacting a parable that was to have its historical fulfilment in the overthrow and dispersion

of the Jewish nation, which, even under the beneficent treatment of the Divine Husbandman, bore no fruit (Mark xi. 13).

583. The Ascension of Christ is generally supposed to have taken place from some point on Olivet, and a church now stands on the traditional spot. But the evangelist Luke says "He led them out as far as Bethany," and Dean Stanley has suggested to a place between the mountain and the village. "On the wild uplands which immediately overhang the village" writes the Dean, "He finally withdrew from the eyes of His disciples, in a seclusion which, perhaps, could nowhere else be found so near the stir of a mighty city" (Luke xxiv. 50).

JERUSALEM TO JERICHO.

584. After leaving Bethany, past which it runs, the road from Jerusalem to Jericho threads its course up-hill and down dale, amongst rugged hills covered here and there with thorn-bushes and beds of stone. In our Lord's time it was a well-frequented route used by the Jews from Galilee and travellers from the east, journeying to and from Jerusalem.

585. On the road to Jericho from Bethany is the BIR-EL-KHAT or "Apostles' Well," where by the side of a small ruined Khan or Inn, a spring of clear sweet water, under a Saracenic arch, pours into a trough. Among the thousands of travellers who have quenched their thirst at this well we may confidently number Christ and His Disciples. It has been identified as the En-Shemesh, or "Spring of the Sun" mentioned in Joshua xviii. 17.

586. Beyond the "Apostles' Well," on the right of the road to Jericho, is the little valley of the Sidr-tree—the "Spina Christi." Here lie the ruins of the Khan Hathrur. These ruins may not be ancient, but they probably stand on the site of an older Khan; and it is an impressive thought that our Lord may Himself have rested at the Khan Hathrur; above all, that He may have rested there for the last time when on His way to Jerusalem on the Friday before His crucifixion. There is nothing to make it unlikely that He

referred to this ancient way-side inn, in the Parable of the Good Samaritan (Luke x. 34).

587. Where the road from Jerusalem ends, the Wady-Kelt, "a thread of verdure at the bottom of a deep glen," marks the course and outlet of the torrent now called the "Kelt," which some think was the brook Cherith that was "before Jordan," where, by command of God, Elijah hid himself from the wrath of Ahab, and was fed by ravens (1 Kings xvii. 2-7).

588. The Wady-Kelt is a deep and wide ravine, at the end of which the traveller finds himself in front of a precipice, perhaps 500 feet high, pierced by many caverns. "We gaze down into the ravine," writes Dr. Tristram, "and see the ravens, eagles, and griffon-vultures sailing beneath us, monarchs of the waste indeed, but the necessary 'sanitary commissioners' of the district provided by nature."

589. From the top of the gorge-like end of the Wady-Kelt, one of the finest views in southern Palestine is obtained. Directly below, the desolate plain divides it from the Jordan. Beyond, and a little higher, are the Plains of Moab, where Israel encamped before crossing to the Promised Land. Beyond these rise the mountains of Moab, one of them being Pisgah, from the top of which Moses saw the land for which he had longed and striven, but was never to enter (Deut. xxxiv. 1-4).

590. At the north of the Wady-Kelt, in the wilderness, is MOUNT QUARANTANIA, the supposed scene of our Lord's temptation and forty-days' fast. To the south-east lie the calm waters of the Dead Sea.

591. In the sides of Mount Quarantania are tiers of cells long used as dwellings by Christian hermits, and even now by visitors from eastern lands. On the ceilings and walls of many of these cells, frescoes of our Lord and of events in His life are to be seen.

592. Besides the torrent-stream of the Wady-Kelt, two living springs "rise out of the foot of the limestone range, and enrich the Plain of Jericho—one now, as always, called "Dûk"; the other, and larger, as well as the more celebrated, called the "Spring of Elisha." The waters of this

spring were probably those which the prophet "healed" (2 Kings ii. 19-22).

593. From the mouth of the Wady-Kelt the PLAIN OF JERICHO extended eastward to the Jordan—a "green circle of tangled thickets," having a rich soil, a plentiful water-supply, and, during a large portion of the year, a tropical climate. Its forest of palms was eight miles in length and three miles in breadth, and stretching through its open spaces were corn-fields, olive groves, and fruit gardens.

JERICHO AND DISTRICT.

594. **Jericho** stood at the western side of the Plain which still bears its name, where the Spring of Elisha and its sister Spring rise, and where the torrent of the Wady-Kelt bursts through the mountain opening. The Arab hamlet, Er-Riha, a wretched collection of hovels, marks the site of the ancient City of Palms, "high and fenced up to heaven," the capital of the Valley of the Jordan, and the key of southern Palestine.

595. With a singularly fortunate position, a fertile soil, and a tropical climate, ancient Jericho possessed every element of prosperity. "As Joshua witnessed it," writes Dean Stanley, "it must have recalled to him the magnificent palm groves of Egypt; to his lean and war-worn host it must have been a tempting sight, giving a visible assurance that the land promised to their fathers by Jehovah was indeed a 'land flowing with milk and honey.'

596. Jericho and its district are intimately associated with the prophets Elijah and Elisha. They came to Jericho from Bethel and went from it to the banks of the Jordan while the sons of the prophets stood "afar off." Near it were the spot where Elijah was "taken up" in the chariot of fire, and Abel-Meholah, "the Meadow of the Dance," where Elisha was first seen behind his oxen when Elijah passed northward from the desert of Sinai on his way to Damascus (2 Kings ii. 7; 2 Kings ii. 11; 1 Kings xix. 16).

597. In the time of the Crusades, the sugar-cane was grown near the Spring of Elisha, in the Plain of Jericho,

and some portions of the sugar-mills and their aqueducts still remain. The sugar thence derived was believed by some to be the "wild honey" which formed part of the food of John the Baptist (Matt. iii. 4; Mark i. 6).

598. Josephus states that the groves of palms and gardens of balsam in the Jericho district were rich sources of revenue, and were once given by Antony to Cleopatra. They were so valuable indeed that Herod the Great afterwards redeemed them for his own benefit.

599. The great value of the palm and balsam revenues in the Jericho district enable us to understand how it came to pass that the Romans appointed collectors of customs there. Their usage was to appoint common tax-gatherers, like Levi, and superintendents or supervisors like Zacchæus.

600. The centuries which have flown since our Lord entered and passed through Jericho have completely changed the aspect of the district. There are few if any palms and balsams now; the trees have disappeared, so completely, indeed, that a solitary relic of the ancient palm-forest, seen so late as the year 1838 near Jericho, has gone. No wonder that the less numerous sycamore-figs should have vanished.

601. When Christ came from Ephraim to Jerusalem to be present at the Passover, His route lay along the border-line of Galilee and Samaria, which led through the city of Jericho, and He probably travelled with some caravan of pilgrims going to the capital with the same purpose. Josephus says the road ran among palm-groves and gardens of balsam, and that the *sycamore-fig* tree which flourished in the district was not unfrequently planted in the middle of the road.

602. Reaching Jericho on His way from Ephraim to Jerusalem our Lord gave sight to a well-known beggar named Bartimæus, who sat at the gate of the city—a miracle of mercy which deeply impressed the inhabitants of Jericho and increased His fame in the land (Mark x. 46-52).

603. It is not improbable that Zacchæus witnessed the miracle wrought upon blind Bartimæus at the gate of Jericho, and received from it the deep impression which prompted him to climb a sycamore-fig tree in order to obtain a good

view of the Great Healer, and also led to the salvation of himself and his household (Luke xix. 4).

604. All that we know of Zacchæus of Jericho is contained in Luke's Gospel. Tradition, however, always ready to canonize the first friends of Christ, made the little superintendent of taxes into a bishop, and he appears in church records as Bishop of Cæsarea. The Syrian relic-makers and sight-showers point out a tower which stands in the village of Riha, near Jericho, as the house of Zacchæus.

605. The term in the original Greek of the New Testament which designates the office held by Zacchæus implies that he was the superintendent of customs in and around Jericho, having a commission from his Roman principal to collect the taxes levied on the Jews by the Romans, and who, in the execution of that trust, employed subordinates who were accountable to him, as he was accountable to his superior, whether that official resided at Rome, or, as was more likely, in the district itself.

606. The office of superintendent or supervisor of taxes under the Romans was a profitable one. He who held it could make money because he "farmed" the taxes. Zacchæus probably did so; hence the evangelist's words in describing him—"and he was rich" (Luke xix. 2).

607. There is no reason to suppose, as some do, that Zacchæus was a Gentile. He was a "son of Abraham." Hence the intense dislike of him cherished by the Pharisees and stricter Jews, who hated every man that accepted employment as a tax-gatherer in the service of their Roman conquerors, and always classed them with the vile and the immoral. Publicans were always associated with sinners (Luke xix. 9).

608. The range of white limestone hills that rises behind Jericho—weird, treeless, barren—is supposed to be the scene of our Lord's temptation and forty-days' fast. Hence the name it received centuries ago, and still bears—the QUARANTANIA. The hill-sides are perforated with caves, in many of which pious hermits have dwelt, attracted by the mystery and sanctity of the locality.

609. It was into the district of the Quarantania that John the Baptist first came preaching repentance. He doubtless lived in some leafy covert, woven of the branches of the Jordan forest, as he chose the dress, habits, and food of his predecessor Elijah (Matthew iii. 4; Mark i. 6).

610. Two miles from Jericho a mound now marks the sight of ancient GILGAL, and a spring its pool. At this place the Israelites erected a circle of twelve stones to commemorate the passage of the Jordan. No remains of such a sacred ring are to be found; nevertheless, Major Conder believes they did form a kind of Druidical circle or sanctuary (Joshua iv. 20).

611. At Gilgal was the first regular settlement of Israel in the Promised Land, and the first spot pronounced "holy." There the Tabernacle remained during the long wars in the interior of Palestine, till it found its resting place at Shiloh, and in the sacred grove were celebrated, in later times, the solemn assemblies of Samuel and Saul, and of David on his return from exile.

612. From Gilgal Elisha "went up" the ascent through the pass to Bethel, where, in the forest, now destroyed, lurked the two she-bears; and hence, too, Naaman, at Elisha's command, went down to the Jordan to bathe in the waters which he despised in order to be cleansed of his leprosy (2 Kings ii. 23; 2 Kings v.).

613. The distance from the site of Jericho to the river Jordan is about five miles. The track is along the last miles of the Wady-Kelt—a broad watercourse strewn with boulders and shingles, with banks 20 to 30 feet high, fringed with stunted thorn-bushes. The Plain of Jericho becomes little better than a succession of mounds of salt-marl on which nothing grows. But there is one spring on the way, that of Beth-Hogla, "home of partridges," with pure bright water which carries life wherever it flows.

614. The country on the other side Jordan opposite the Plain of Jericho was called SHITTIM. There Joshua encamped the Israelites to prepare for the crossing of the Jordan. From Shittim he sent the two spies to "view the land and Jericho," to whom, when they were pursued by the

men of Jericho, the "harlot Rahab" gave shelter, hiding them under stalks of flax on the roof of her house (Joshua ii.).

615. It was during a flood-time, when a great volume of water poured along the river bed, that the Israelites quitted their encampments at Shittim and crossed over the Jordan, at a place "right against Jericho," as described in the third chapter of the Book of Joshua. "And it came to pass, when the people removed from their tents to pass over Jordan, the priests that bare the ark of the covenant, being before the people; and when they that bare the ark were come unto Jordan, and the feet of the priests that bare the ark were dipped in the brink of the water (for Jordan overfloweth its banks all the time of harvest), that the waters which came down from above stood, and rose up in one heap, a great way off at Adam, the city that is beside Zaretan: and those that went down toward the sea of the Arabah, even the Salt Sea, were wholly cut off: and the people passed over right against Jericho" (Joshua iii. 14-16).

616. The passage of the Jordan by the Israelites was a stupendous miracle. The full bed of the river was dried before them; and not for a short space, but for a distance of 30 miles northward even to a place called ADAM, near Zaretan; between this crossing-place and the Dead Sea the waters "failed and were cut off." Thus the people who numbered more than two millions were not confined to a single point but could pass over at any part of the empty channel.

617. ZARETAN, near which was Adam, the place to which the bed of the Jordan was dried to allow the Israelites to pass over, is probably Zartan, near the hill of Sartabeh, where Solomon had brazen vessels made for his Temple, as the soil of that part of the Ghor is said to be specially fitted for the work of making moulds.

618. After crossing over Jordan, the Israelites invested Jericho for six days according to the command of God. On the seventh day the armed host compassed the city seven times, the priests blew with the trumpets, the people gave a great shout, the wall of the city fell down, and the one great fortress which barred their entrance into the Promised Land fell into their hands (Joshua vi.).

THE DEAD SEA.

619. The Jordan empties itself into the **Dead Sea**, the most curious and remarkable of inland seas on the surface of the globe. It is 1,292 feet below the level of the Mediterranean Sea, and the most depressed sheet of water in the world. It has no outlet; evaporation is the only visible means of removing its superfluous water. It is variously called the Dead Sea, the Sea of Sodom, the sea of the Plain, and the Lake Asphaltites.

620. The cavity of the Dead Sea was probably caused by the same great natural convulsion which shook Palestine to its centre and depressed the Valley of the Jordan, a convulsion which took place long before historical times. From the level of the Plain of Jericho to its southern shore is a descent of 500 feet. The length of this sea is 53 miles and its greatest breadth 10 miles.

621. The presence at the south-eastern end of the Dead Sea of a ridge of rock salt 300 feet high and five miles in length, an extraordinary quantity of saline matter, and a never-ceasing process of evaporation, combine to produce the excessive saltness of its water. "The bed of the Sea," writes Dr. George Adam Smith, "appears to be covered with salt crystals. Nauseous to the taste, the water is very brilliant; seen from far away, no lake looks more blue and beautiful."

622. The buoyancy of the water of the Dead Sea is well-known; it is difficult to sink the limbs in swimming. If you throw a stick on to the surface it seems to rest there as on a mirror, so little of it actually penetrates the water. Dr. Smith contradicts every statement that fish live in it. He says, "No fish live in its waters, nor is it proved that any low forms of life have been discovered in them."

623. The strange, weird borders of the Dead Sea are "symbols of forsakenness and desolation." A low beach of gravel is broken twice on the western side by mountain cliffs that come down to the sea, and once on the eastern side by a curious peninsula six miles wide called "El-Lisan," or "The Tongue," formed of steep banks of marl from 40

to 60 feet high. Above the beach is an almost continuous hedge of drift-wood, dead and bleached, spangled with salt. Above this again rise terraces of marl and precipitous mountains bare and barren.

624. "In this awful hollow of the Ghor, this bit of the infernal regions come up to the surface," as Dr. G. A. Smith describes it, the Cities of the Plain—Sodom, Gomorrah—were destroyed because of their terrible wickedness. "And Jehovah rained upon Sodom and upon Gomorrah brimstone and fire from the Lord out of heaven; and He overthrew those cities, and all the Plain, and all the inhabitants of the cities, and that which grew upon the ground." Where these cities stood is a matter of uncertainty and of continued controversy (Genesis xix. 24-25).

625. In the general destruction of human life which made the overthrow of the Cities of the Plain the most awful tragedy in Old Testament history, it pleased God to provide for the escape from Sodom, in which they lived, of the patriarch Lot and his family. The merciful message brought by the angels, Lot's natural hesitation to act upon it, the unbelief of his sons-in-law, and probably, too, of his wife, are described in the 19th chapter of Genesis. At length Lot entreated to be allowed to flee to, and remain in Zoar. This request granted, and the fugitives well on their way, the mysterious work of Divine retribution began. "But," runs the Bible story, "Lot's wife looked back from behind him, and she became a pillar of salt" (Genesis xix. 26).

626. On the southern side of the Dead Sea are found needles or pillars of rock, more or less isolated, which atmospheric influences are detaching from the masses of mineral salt. These remarkable objects help to keep alive the story of Lot's wife, who was changed into a pillar of salt while lingering to look back upon Sodom during its destruction. The Arab legend still current in the district differs little from the Bible narrative (Genesis xix. 26).

627. In his work, "The Desert of the Exodus," Mr. E. H. Palmer describes the most impressive of the "Pillars of Salt," called by the Arabs "Bint Sheikh Lot," or "Lot's wife," as "a tall isolated needle of rock, which does really bear a curious resemblance to an Arab woman, with a child

upon her shoulders." The "Bint Sheikh Lot" stands upon the edge of a plateau, a thousand feet above the Dead Sea.

628. About ten miles down the eastern side of the Dead Sea, south of Pisgah, "frowning over a wild gorge," are the ruins of the Castle of Machærus, where Herod Antipas imprisoned and beheaded John the Baptist. It was while in this dungeon John sent messengers to Jesus asking, in some doubt and perhaps discouragement, the question "Art Thou He that should come, or look we for another?" (Matthew xi. 3).

629. At the mouth of the wild gorge, overlooked by the Castle of Machærus, amongst rushing waters veiled by oleanders, lay Callirhoë with its famous hot springs, where Herod the Great nearly died when carried over to try the baths, and whence he had to be got back as best might be to Jericho, to breathe his last there a few days after.

RIVERS FLOWING FROM THE EAST INTO THE JORDAN.

630. Flowing eastward through Moab to the Dead Sea, about 25 miles south of the Plain of Jordan is the river ARNON. Flowing eastward from Ammon, about 25 miles north of the Plain of Jordan is the River JABBOK; flowing in the same direction from Gilead into the Jordan, about five miles below the southern border of the Sea of Galilee, is the river YARMUK. These three rivers are the only considerable streams that come from the mountains east of the Jordan.

631. The ARNON, which is not far from Machærus, was the first considerable stream crossed by the Israelites on their way from the Desert of the Wanderings to the Land of Promise. With the passage of the Arnon their period of conflict began, their first foe being Sihon, King of the Amorites (Numbers xxi. 21-24).

632. Although the source of the JABBOK is only 18 miles east of the Valley of Jordan, it has a round-about course of over 60 miles, winding northward through a desert country, then west-south-west towards the Jordan into which it falls.

Its valley is of great fertility. The peculiar colour of the water of this river—a grey olive—gives to it its modern name Zerka.

633. It was across the ford of the Jabbok, and at night, Jacob took his two wives, his two handmaidens, and his eleven children, after he had sent forward a costly peace-offering to his angry brother Esau. Left alone at midnight "there wrestled a man with him until the breaking of the day." Conscious that this mysterious experience was a Divine manifestation he called the name of the place "Peni-el," "for," said he, "I have seen God face to face and my life is preserved." During that midnight struggle Jacob's name was changed to Israel (Genesis xxxii. 30).

634. In Moab, Heshbon, Ammon, and Gilead, many rude stone monuments are found, the uses of which were partly historical and partly worshipful. At present the Moabite Stone is the only important inscription from this region. It was found accidentally by a missionary, just as the inscription on one of the walls of the Pool of Siloam was found by a Jewish boy. Jacob and Saul and other Hebrew heroes erected such memorials.

635. The river YARMUK flows through a gorge or ravine of limestone bearing traces of its primeval volcanic origin. Dr. Tristram traversed its course, desiring to find the hot springs which were said to exist near it. He found one, the character of the water being similar to that of the hot baths at Tiberias.

PERÆA.

636. In our Lord's time the whole country lying between the river Arnon in the south and the Yarmuk in the north was called PERÆA, which means the land over, or beyond, or across—the country on the other side Jordan.

637. The Jews always regarded Peræa, Galilee, and Judæa as the three Jewish provinces, and Samaria as a foreign or at least an alien province, through which they would not pass; so, when travelling from Galilee to the south, they crossed the Jordan by some northern ford, probably that at Beth-Abarah, thus making the journey, as they considered, on purely Jewish soil.

638. Our Lord must frequently have been in Peræa, if only to pass through it on His way to Jerusalem. It was the chief, perhaps the sole scene of the labours of the Seventy, whom He sent out to preach after the missionary work of the Twelve in Galilee. The names of none of the places visited by the Seventy are recorded, but they were probably the larger towns near the route to Jerusalem (Luke x. 1).

639. On His way from Ephraim to Jerusalem, our Lord met and healed ten lepers; little children were brought to Him, whom He blest; and the rich young ruler came to Him to know how he might inherit eternal life. On that journey also He spake the parables of the unjust judge and the labourers in the vineyard; answered the question of the Pharisee about divorce; addressed the disciples upon the dangers incident to riches; and in reply to Peter, He spake of the rewards that should be given to the Twelve and to all faithful disciples (Matt. xix.).

DECAPOLIS.

640. North of Peræa and for some distance intermingled with it was the "**Region of Decapolis**," in which, as its name implies, were the ten cities that had formed a league, and had acquired special rights and privileges not granted to, or obtained by, other communities. The names of the original cities of this famous league were Bethshan or Scythopolis, the only one on the west side of the Jordan; Pella, Gadara, Hippos, Philadelphia, Gerasa, Dion, Canatha, Raphana, and Damascus.

641. That many of the inhabitants of Decapolis were heathens we know from their pagan worship, customs, and habits. They bred swine which Jews dare not do, and Matthew, describing the effect of our Lord's teaching upon the people of that region, says "they glorified the God of Israel," thereby indicating that they came to glorify Jehovah in place of their former deities (Matt. xv. 31).

642. Christ is reported to have taught and done mighty works in Decapolis. Mark says that the man who had been delivered of the legion of evil spirits at Gergesa "departed

and began to publish in Decapolis how great things Jesus had done for him; and the same evangelist mentions an extensive tour taken by our Lord "through the midst of the coasts of Decapolis" (Mark v. 20; Mark vii. 31).

643. The scene of the feeding of the five thousand at the north-eastern end of the Sea of Galilee was in Decapolis; the scene of the second great similar miracle—the feeding of the four thousand—was also in Decapolis, probably on the south-eastern side of the sea in the neighbourhood of the ravine now called Wady-Semak, opposite Mejdel, the site of ancient Magdala.

PHŒNICIAN SITES AND CITIES.

644. A little north of Beirout is an old military road along which Roman armies have passed; and in the country around it—part of the ancient PHŒNICIA—are remains of stone tablets and pillars bearing inscriptions that tell of Sennacherib, Esarhaddon, Shalmaneser, Tiglath Pileser, Rameses II of Egypt,—the Pharaoh of the Hebrew bondage,—and Nebuchadnezzar of Babylon.

645. From Beirout to SIDON, the oldest city of Phœnicia, is a wearisome journey, through miles of deep sand, past wild mountainous headlands, and across rough water-courses, not easily traversed.

646. SIDON is beautifully situated amidst gardens and orchards where grow pomegranates, almonds, palms, bananas, apricots, figs, olives, plums, pears, peaches, cherries, and oranges; large quantities of these fruits, especially of oranges, are sent inland to Damascus.

647. Sidon is in the portion of Palestine originally assigned to the tribe of Asher, but Asher never really obtained it, because the tribe did not drive out the Canaanites. The people of Asher had therefore to dwell amongst the idolaters.

648. Sidon lost its pride of place when, about 1,200 years before Christ, it was taken by the Philistines. Then Tyre became the first Phœnician City.

649. Isaiah speaks of the merchants of Sidon, and Ezekiel refers to the fame of its sailors. Its timber-hewers had a great repute in the time of Solomon.

650. The "COAST OF TYRE AND SIDON" visited by our Lord was in all probability the plain of Sidon, a long sweep of sea-coast on which Tyre and Sidon stood.

651. It was to the coast of Tyre and Sidon our Lord went with his disciples to secure a season of retirement, alike from public labour and public observation, before entering upon the last and most arduous portion of His ministry.

652. While in Phœnicia our Lord was recognised by a woman of the country and, at her earnest entreaty, despite the attempts of the disciples to send her away on the ground that she was a heathen, and, in their estimation, no better than a dog, He healed her daughter, and so taught them that all men are God's children, and that God answers the prayer of faith by whomsoever it is presented (Matt. xv. 22-28).

653. While on its way to Rome the ship in which the Apostle Paul sailed as a prisoner touched at Sidon, and he was allowed to go ashore. There he met a band of Christian converts, amongst whom he found friends (Acts xxvii. 3).

654. In Sidon, as elsewhere in Syria and the East, sacred mottoes are to be seen on the outside of some of the houses. It was because of this custom Moses said to the Israelites, "These words which I have commanded thee this day thou shalt write upon the posts of thy house and on thy gates"; God's words, not words honouring idols (Deut. vi. 6-9).

655. Tyre and Sidon were famous from the earliest ages for their dye works, in which was manufactured a purple dye held in the highest esteem throughout the then civilized world.

656. The State-robes of emperors and kings were sometimes, indeed still are, dyed purple, the famous Tyrian colour. Hence, royal children are said to have been "born in the purple," and when a monarch has ascended a throne he is said to have "assumed the purple."

657. The purple dye of Tyre and Sidon was obtained from two species of shell-fish found on the Phœnician coast.

Although they are now all but extinct in the shallow water, whole masses of them are, at times, thrown up from the sea during storms.

658. The shell-fish yielding purple dye at Tyre and Sidon are at first of a whitish colour, but when exposed to light they become yellow and then green, and finally, according to species, red or purple.

659. There runs down from the interior to refresh and enrich Sidon, a stream called the Zaherany. It flows from a copious spring far up in the mountains, known as the "Fountain of the Cup." Going from Sidon with this stream the traveller soon reaches the site of Sarepta.

660. Paul landed at Tyre on his way from Greece to Jerusalem, and tarried there seven days. When leaving it, its disciples in Tyre accompanied him some part of his way; at parting, they "kneeled down and prayed" (Acts xxi. 5).

661. Tyre is a place of ruins. Ezekiel's prophecy has indeed been fulfilled; for the fisherman spreads his nets on the ruined walls, and the once famous "Queen of the Sea" is only a fishing-village with a small trade in cereals, fruit, and milk.

662. The River Leontes pours itself into the sea about half-way between Sarepta and Tyre. It is 120 miles long, and it descends fully 4,000 feet in its course from the mountains of Lebanon.

663. SAREPTA lies near the sea, and is well and pleasantly situated. In the Hebrew Bible it is called Zarpath, which means "melting houses," because it was a chief centre of the glass manufacture in Phœnicia.

664. The chief interest of Sarepta lies in its connection with the prophet Elijah. A spot is still shown at the old harbour where a Christian church once stood, on the alleged site of the widow's house in which Elijah lived (1 Kings xvii.).

665. The LEBANON RANGE OF MOUNTAINS may be called the northern boundary and barrier of Palestine. With their valleys and ledges and lower spurs they constitute the Lebanon country, which is the home of the people, known as the Druses, who number about 80,000.

666. MOUNT HERMON is the most famous mountain in the Lebanon. It has three peaks, the highest of which is called in Scripture "the lofty height." The inhabitants call it "Jebel-es-Sheikh"—the mountain of the white-haired patriarch."

667. The Transfiguration of our Lord and Saviour Jesus Christ took place on one of the plateaus of Hermon in the Lebanon range, probably near Cæsarea Philippi. Which of the heights witnessed the revelation of the Lord's glory is unknown.

668. It is certain that by one of the passes in the Lebanon Abraham pursued king Chedorlaomer and his allies from Dan to Damascus (Genesis xiv. 14-15); it is probable, also, that the Apostle Paul crossed this mountain-land on his memorable journey to the Syrian capital (Acts ix. 2).

669. CÆSAREA PHILIPPI was the little town of Banias, enlarged and adorned by Herod the Great, and also by his son Philip, the tetrarch, who called it Cæsarea in honour of the Emperor Tiberius Cæsar. It must not be confounded with Cæsarea on the coast of Samaria.

670. The situation of Cæsarea Philippi is unique. The town nestles in a recess at the southern base of the "Mighty Hermon," whose peaks rise in majesty to a height of 7,000 and even 8,000 feet.

671. It was when He came unto the coasts of Cæsarea Philippi our Lord put to His disciples the questions, "Whom do men say that I the Son of Man am?" and "Whom say ye that I am?" and on receiving Peter's answer "Thou art the Christ, the Son of the living God," said to him, "Thou art Peter, and upon this rock I will build My Church" (Matt. xvi. 13-18).

672. ACRE, on the coast of the Bay of Acre, is a poor place, although it has figured in the military operations of England and France in modern times. In the first chapter of the Book of Judges we learn that it was too strong for the tribe of Asher to capture, in whose portion of Palestine it was.

673. As a fortified haven the town of Akka, or Acre, was valued by the Persian generals as an important basis of

operations in their wars against Egypt. It was also called Ptolemais.

674. Acre, the ancient Ptolemais, is most noteworthy to Christians as the place at which the Apostle Paul landed when he went up to Jerusalem for the last time, saluting the brethren then in the town, and staying with them one day.

675. Acre contains about 8,000 inhabitants. Its staple trade is the exportation of corn. Long trains of camels laden with grain from the interior may be seen any morning waiting for entrance at the city gate.

676. The trains of camels bearing corn from eastern Syria have always passed over the road behind Nazareth on their way to Acre. Our Lord must often have seen them, and they may have suggested to Him the wider world and the sheep of the other and larger flocks beyond Palestine which had claims upon His loving care.

677. Besides the Leontes, the Hasbany, and the Upper Part of the Jordan, only two other rivers in Northern Galilee possess historical interest, namely, the N'AMAN and the KISHON.

678. The river N'AMAN rises in the mountains north-east of the village of Shefa 'Omr where are perennial fountains, the waters of which are used to drive a number of mills. The length of the N'aman from the fountains to the Bay of Acre is less than six miles.

679. The little river N'aman is the ancient Belus, mentioned by Pliny, who repeats the story of the discovery of glass by some sailors who were cooking their dinner on the sand at the river's mouth. Dr. Thomson says there are vitreous rocks in the district, and suggests that if the sailors supported their sauce-pans on pieces of such rock placed round the fire, the melted rock mixing with the sand might have given the first hint which led to the discovery.

680. The river KISHON has its source at En-Gannin, now called Ain-Jenin, the most important town between Nablus and Nazareth. The Kishon is mentioned in the "song" which Deborah and Barak sang, after the defeat and murder of Sisera. "The stars in their courses fought against Sisera.

The river Kishon swept them away, that ancient river, the river Kishon" (Judges v. 20-21).

681. Like nearly all the streams in Northern Palestine, the Kishon loses most of its water in the dry season. It is only a permanent stream indeed for a few miles, and is one of the shortest historical rivers in the world.

682. It was to "THE BROOK KISHON" that the people brought the prophets of Baal from Mount Carmel, at the command of Elijah, and slew them; thereby enacting one of the strangest tragedies recorded in the Bible (1 Kings xviii. 40).

Brook & Hinchliffe, Printers, Manchester.

www.ingramcontent.com/pod-product-compliance
Lightning Source LLC
Chambersburg PA
CBHW022141160426
43197CB00009B/1377